NEXT YEAR
IN
JERUSALEM

NEXT YEAR
IN
JERUSALEM

by Avital Shcharansky
with Ilana Ben-Josef

*Translated from the Russian by
Stefani Hoffman*

William Morrow and Company, Inc.
New York   1979

Library of Congress Cataloging in Publication Data

Shcharansky, Avital.
  Next year in Jerusalem.

  1. Shcharansky, Avital. 2. Shcharansky, Anatoly. 3. Israel—Emigration and immigration—Biography. 4. Jews in Russia—Biography. 5. Jews in Russia—Persecutions. 6. Russia—Emigration and immigration—Biography. I. Ben-Josef, Ilana, joint author. II. Title.
JV8749.P3S555   325'.247'095694   [B]   79-17494
ISBN 0-688-03552-3

Book Design by Michael Mauceri

Printed in the United States of America.

First Edition

1 2 3 4 5 6 7 8 9 10

Contents

NEXT YEAR
IN
JERUSALEM

Arkhipov Street

The street caught me by surprise. It was small, narrow and crooked, with few buildings, mostly nondescript except for a very strange one with high columns. The Hebrew inscription on a blue border below the cornice gave it an air of mystery. Children often played soccer in the small square opposite it. Keeping their distance from the synagogue's officious presence, young Jews stood on the narrow sidewalk near the wire-enclosed square. In small groups or individually, they talked animatedly, frequently mentioning the words "visa" and "invitation."

At first glance, the police sentry booth to the left of the synagogue steps seemed out of place, but its purpose became clear on Saturdays. When the Jews gathered on the other side of the street, the K.G.B. agents thronged around the sentry booth. They carefully watched the scene opposite them, or mixed with the crowd of Jews in order to overhear conversations. Sometimes they became more aggressive; suddenly, without any apparent reason, they headed toward someone. Like a school of sharks, slow and silent, they crossed the street, surrounded their victim and led him away to the puzzled silence of bystanders.

I first chanced on this street in October 1973, during the

Yom Kippur War. The weather was awful: snow fell slowly in large sticky flakes from low leaden clouds and turned into mud on the ground. Although the cold was bone-chilling, people stood around for hours. New arrivals would ask:

"*Nu*, where are we now?"

"We're advancing toward Damascus."

"What about down south, in the Sinai?"

Meter by meter, the situation on every front was discussed with such knowledge and assurance that it was as if every one of these Moscow Jews were sitting in a tank or commanding the general staff. The anxious mood was tempered by certainty that "we" would win. Neither the snow, nor the dark silhouettes on the opposite side of the street, nor the radios and newspapers accusing Israel of the most unbelievable sins and atrocities and heralding her defeat could have any effect. We felt as if we were a part of Israel; we were almost there.

I was then living with my brother Michael in a small room belonging to Ilana and Benjamin, close friends who had left for Israel. Ilana and Benjamin sent us letters, postcards and photographs filled with sunshine. They warmed our gloomy abode, whose sole furnishings consisted of two mattresses and my drafting board, which also served as a table. I was studying art then and spent my time sketching and visiting museums. My eyes were directed more to the outside world than within. That was probably why I wasn't much affected by the dissident activities and Zionism of some of my friends. Although I already planned to go to Israel, my decision to do this was unclear to me. If someone had asked me why, I couldn't have answered. I felt stifled in a dark world and I wanted to break out of it. Whenever I heard or read about Israel, my imagination sketched bright, vibrant pictures. Now living in Israel and recalling this, I am amazed at how correct my premonitions were.

At that time, my brother had already submitted the documents to emigrate. Not anticipating any trouble, we were surprised when he was thrown out of his job and refused a visa. A period of appeals, requests, letters to various authorities, began; we received no answers.

One morning, I noticed that my brother was dressing very strangely: he put on several sweaters, a scarf, which he never wore, and warm socks. Without answering my puzzled glance, he gave me a note with his friend's telephone number "just in case." Later that day, as I was riding the bus along Tversky Boulevard, I saw a strange and unusual scene: in the very heart of town, under the large TASS sign, stood poorly but warmly dressed young people forming a human chain. They were surrounded by a large number of official visored caps and shoulder boards. It resembled some kind of battle formation, but why wasn't anyone moving? What was the meaning of this strange tableau? Suddenly to my horror I discovered that my brother, rising above everyone, was leading this curious rank.

At that moment placards were lifted up into the air: "Visas instead of prisons!" "Let me go to Israel!" This brought the shoulder boards and official caps into motion. I began banging on the door and screaming for the driver to let me off, but the bus drove past. The last thing I saw was a man jumping in a funny way as he tried to tear the placard away from my brother, who kept on raising it higher and higher. I jumped off the bus and rushed frantically back, noticing nothing in my path. By the time I arrived, no one was there. I looked in the TASS agency and in the neighboring courtyard: nothing. I probably looked very suspicious at that moment against the peaceful gray stream of citizens.

That night, not expecting my brother, I remembered the note with the telephone number. The person I reached was Leva Liberman, my brother's friend, another "refusenik," who came over to see me from the other side of Moscow. He explained that my brother had probably been arrested, but it wasn't yet clear where he was. He calmed me down and suggested that if I would go to the synagogue on Arkhipov

Street and ask around, someone there might be able to help me. As I approached the synagogue the next day, I saw Liberman's flitting figure, the lapels of his plastic raincoat flapping up and down. He greeted me warmly, led me to a group of young people and noisily began introducing me.

Many of them had just served fifteen days in prison for a previous demonstration. They gave me the addresses of several preliminary detention prisons in Moscow where my brother might be and urged me not to panic. They transmitted their calmness to me.

The last person to whom Leva introduced me was Tolik [1] —young, short, in a long dark coat and large hat. He looked at me with cheerful eyes, smiled warmly and said jokingly:

"I am really called Natan. That's what I'll be called in Israel. Are you planning to go?"

"Yes."

"Are you studying Hebrew?"

"I began by myself but wasn't so successful. Is it really possible?"

"Why not? Everyone you see here is studying Hebrew."

"I really want to. Could you help me?"

"I think so. What level are you on?"

"What about you?"

"Well, I already know a thousand words; that's not bad."

I suddenly felt that I wanted terribly to study with him.

"That's it, I'm on the same level," I burst out.

"Good, I'll ask my *moreh* [2] about you, but we study very seriously. You'll have to speak only in Hebrew."

I knew that he was a refusenik like my brother. He had just served fifteen days in prison and had a terrible cold. The wind blew down the street as if through a funnel and he shivered slightly. There was something unusual about him; given his background, he seemed especially remark-

[1] A diminutive of Anatoly.
[2] Teacher in Hebrew.

able: his movements, glance and thoughts suggested freedom. That freedom which in the West is received as a birthright is achieved in Russia only by very rare people, through great spiritual effort. As a result, it appears as "freedom in spite of slavery." Tolik, however, possessed it as a divine gift. He was born that way, and, as I later came to see, he would never change for anything. It's really a talent to be free in a world of denunciations and police agents, where the average citizen gets used to a "double way of life," to "doublethink," or to a "two-faced conscience." When I looked at Tolik for the first time, I thought, Israelis probably look like him.

A few days later, I went to my first Hebrew lesson with great excitement. Several young men and one girl were assembled in the apartment of one of the students. The teacher came in. I later learned that he had been a refusenik for several years. He had not known a word of Hebrew, but through hard work had become one of the best teachers. He had perfected his knowledge of the language by very primitive methods: somewhere he had managed to get hold of a dictionary, and taught himself several thousand words. And somehow he had met some old men who knew how to read the prayerbook with an Ashkenazic accent. Also he had had occasional success in catching the Voice of Israel broadcasts, which provided him with a lot of material. In addition, tourists came with records of Hebrew songs, and these were widely circulated.

His language classes sometimes resembled training for sports. Sitting in front of the television, he tried to translate the newscaster's every word into Hebrew. It was like an obstacle course. First he got warm and had to take off his jacket, then his sweater, and finally, exhausted, he sat facing the screen in only his undershirt with the sweat streaming from his arms. As a reward for it all, it was a pleasure to hear his Hebrew!

We all sat down around a large table and spread out our "textbooks": someone had gotten hold of a children's book from Israel with big letters and funny pictures. One girl had a solid-looking book with engravings. One of the drawings depicted a benevolent-looking bearded man who was supporting his aged teacher. Just able to put the letters together, I read the unfamiliar name below: Joshua Ben-Nun. From that time on, I felt a special, personal relationship to that hero.

The teacher displayed a section of an Israeli newspaper with the text of some Knesset speeches. Tolik had gotten hold of the declension-table cards; he was interested in the structure of the language. Then each student read a prepared piece and everyone discussed the mistakes. When my turn came, I maintained an embarrassed silence and pretended that I could prepare something similar for the next lesson.

When the class was over, the teacher proposed dividing up the roles and holding a Knesset session. I got Shulamit Aloni. Everyone laughed that I, numb from nervousness and incomprehension, should play the role of this dynamic woman, who always commented heatedly on everyone else's speeches. The room was getting warmer, and we were shouting as in a real Knesset session, discussing the problem of the birthrate in Israel, and no one noticed that it was already midnight.

On the way home, Tolik invited me to go with him to his friend's; someone there was leaving for Israel the next day. The apartment door was half open, with people crowding the entrance, the corridor and the kitchen. Although many people there were unacquainted, everyone treated each other warmly— like family. With difficulty we made our way into the living room, and I suddenly saw an attractive young lady surrounded by relatives and realized she was going to leave. Her fiancé was waiting for her in Nazareth. His relatives had come to send him a "living" greeting through her and also to say goodbye to her. It was as if that girl were no longer there; everyone was speaking about Lydda Airport, about the first trip around the country, about their relatives "there." And again, although not like the synagogue or the Hebrew class, Israel was nevertheless very nearby.

At the time we met, Tolik had finished his studies at a technological physics institute which trained high-level engineers. It was an almost exclusively male institution near Moscow, which resembled a monastery in its isolation and intensive study program. The authorities took care of this institute in a unique way: they brought poets in official disfavor there to read their verse so that the students wouldn't be lured by the unofficial *samizdat* literature. They arranged evening dances and "supplied young ladies" from other institutes, and didn't send them home until the morning so that no feelings or passions would distract the students from their studies. This institute was "open." It was even considered the brother institute of M.I.T., and no one had to sign any documents or papers regarding secrecy. Nevertheless, when Tolik got his first refusal, he decided that his training might be the cause for it. Yet at that time, many students and even teachers from there had already left for Israel.

Trying to find out the reason for his refusal, Tolik tried to see someone at O.V.I.R.[3] Finally, General Verein, notorious among the refuseniks, saw him and gave him "a Communist general's word of honor," saying that if Tolik and two of his friends would be "quiet" for two months, they would receive visas.

Demonstrations took place but Tolik decided to test "the general's word of honor," and didn't participate. His friends were skeptical, continued to "make noise," to demon-

[3] The division of visas and licenses, where documents for emigration are prepared.

strate, and very soon left for Israel. When a month passed, Tolik again requested an interview at O.V.I.R., and the same director began to hem and haw:

"I don't know why you were refused. Perhaps you were involved in secret work?"

"No."

"Perhaps one of your relatives?"

"No, that's easy to check out!"

"You were given a flat refusal. We are not interested in letting you go."

After that, Tolik didn't miss a single opportunity to make noise. He signed all letters and petitions demanding free emigration, participated in all demonstrations. The word "demonstration" generally suggests a large, noisy crowd, freely marching along the street, waving placards. But the Jewish demonstrations in the winter of 1974 were different. The details were known only to the five to ten despairing young participants and the Western correspondents were notified in advance. One by one, as if out for a walk, they would meet at the designated spot, always in the center of Moscow.

They quickly formed a rank and, in one motion, would raise up the handwritten signs: "Visa to Israel!" Immediately, tens of K.G.B. agents hung on them and tore away the placards. Foreign correspondents would try to photograph this unique sight, but enraged K.G.B. agents would square accounts with them—cameras flew to the ground, film was exposed. Frightened citizens hurried past, pretending that nothing was happening.

Usually only a few minutes passed from the beginning of the demonstration to the time when all the demonstrators were thrown into a van and led off in an unknown direction. Nobody ever knew whether they would be transported to a "detoxifier," where they would be detained for a day, interrogated and released at night, or whether they would be arrested for fifteen days, which was what happened to my brother. They also faced possible exile to Siberia, which happened later to Mark Nashpitz and Boris Tsitlyonok, Tolik's friends and co-demonstrators. And yet they still went —after all, it was a known fact that many of these "despairing ones" did receive visas. My brother, for example, received his relatively quickly.

I, too, soon got acquainted with the detoxifier. I used to think naively that it was where they brought drunks, dragged off the streets. There they would splash them with water, sober them up and let them sleep it off. Apparently it is a very convenient form of arrest, requiring neither a formal order nor any real cause.

Once a group of refuseniks tried to assemble at the Supreme Soviet to hand over a collective letter with questions about the reasons for the refusals. I knew that Tolik would be there. I was anxious about my brother and him, so I decided to go and watch from the sideline.

As soon as I walked out of the subway car, a man appeared next to me and quietly said something to himself in the inner pocket of his coat. At the time it seemed like a strange joke. Another person met me at the top of the escalator and repeated the same stunt. Everything became clear when two men at the exit grabbed me under the arms and dragged me across the street. I resisted, tried to get rid of them, but no one hurried to help me. On this clear, frosty day, the crowd flowed indifferently around us on both sides. I soon saw the bus with the familiar faces of refuseniks nodding to me from the windows. I landed next to Tolik. The bus started up. Tolik joked, "Perhaps they're taking us straight to Sheremetevo Airport? You see, it's possible even without visas!"

In the back seat Dina Beilin assured a frightened woman, who had apparently wound up accidentally in the bus because of her Semitic features, that we were not criminals or thieves. We simply wanted to go to Israel. They refused us. We waited and waited and finally went to the Supreme Soviet to ask when they would ever let us out.

"Look, that's Professor Lerner, a cyberneticist," Dina said, pointing to an elderly, gray-haired man. "He has a daughter and grandchildren in Israel and hasn't been able to see them for many years. And that girl, over there, she certainly doesn't look like a criminal, she just wants to be with her family." The woman quickly calmed down and began to question Dina about Israel and about the obligatory "invitations" from relatives.

Then I heard another "accidental" fellow traveler (I saw how desperately he fought the K.G.B. men when they dragged him onto the bus) who was unable to calm down.

"Why? Why?" he screamed. "I'm an old Bolshevik! I'm not with them! I'm one of yours!"

As we rode, we sang Hebrew songs at the top of our lungs, while the poor "old Bolshevik," thrusting himself out the window, tried to outscream us with a popular Communist jingle from the thirties: "Fly forward, locomotive!/The commune is our only stop."

When the bus stopped at the detoxifier, a thick ring of soldiers encircled us, while the astonished citizens looked out of the neighboring buildings.

"Why did they bring them to a detoxifier? They're not drunks, they're all so intellectual-looking . . ."

"Sober and intellectual," we were brought to a wooden barracks with a long corridor and an endless row of doors. The women were separated from the men, and we ten women were swiftly locked into a room with a barred window, with nothing in it but four beds without mattresses. The women looked at me sympathetically, I was shivering with cold. Now I understood why my brother dressed so warmly before a demonstration. Someone gave me a sweater. Gradually we started talking and spent the day, numb with cold, sitting on the stiff metal beds. About five o'clock in the afternoon, they began to call the men out for interrogation. Through a small window in the door, I saw Tolik pass by. The men were not brought back.

I was called out.

"Your full name? Why did you obstruct street traffic?" and finally, "What is the reason for your detention?"

This was some kind of absurdity. I explained that I did not know why they had detained me, and refused to answer. I couldn't stand keeping up this idiotic game. Because of my stubbornness, they kept me in the room alone until late at night, when, without any explanation, they led me to the exit and went away.

Shivering, hungry, upset and angry, I stood alone in the darkness on an unfamiliar street. Suddenly, a figure moved away from the wall: it was Tolik. He had been standing there for several hours. Shivering from cold and exhaustion, we walked along the dark, empty street, searching vainly for a taxi. To cheer me up, he told me a funny story. For several days he had been followed by a black Volga.[4] Late one night he stopped a taxi and got in the back seat. The young driver noticed that a car was following them. He probably had read a lot of detective stories and fancied himself the hero of one. He zoomed forward and drove like a madman through the empty streets, winding and turning into side streets, glancing back fiercely at his pursuers and chuckling when he succeeded in eluding them. Finally, he got so carried away with himself that he allowed them to get very close. He made a pistol with his fingers, leaned toward the steering wheel and shot from the shoulder: "Bang-bang-bang." They took it seriously. This adventurous soul really got it when they managed to board the taxi and searched the whole car for guns. This guy almost died of fright when he found out who he was playing "chase" with. That was one of the "funny" stories we tried to amuse each other with in those days.

I continued going to the Hebrew lessons. It was torture for me. Each time I found a new excuse to hide my true level from the teacher. I feared most of all that he would

---

[4] The car usually used by K.G.B. agents.

exclude me and I wouldn't be able to meet Tolik there. But little by little, an interest in the language took precedence over my fear and embarrassment. Tolik told me that he knew about my deception, but didn't want to expose me. I couldn't catch up to him, but still, when he took me home at night, it was so nice to speak with him in our primitive Hebrew.

Once a week we met at the home of a refusenik for a *dibur*.[5] Teacher and students spoke uninterruptedly in Hebrew for several hours about everything and anything. The precondition for being there was not to be silent and not to speak a word of Russian. An "offender" had to forfeit his *dibur* until the following week. The conversations were very lively and usually ended with everyone singing Israeli songs.

I was invited to my first Passover Seder at this hospitable home. Like most Soviet Jewish families, mine didn't celebrate Passover. All I knew was that matzoh is eaten. On a glistening, stiffly starched white tablecloth unfamiliar objects with mysterious names appeared: *moror* (bitter herbs), *charoseth, zeroa* (shank bone).

The men put on yarmulkes and our teacher began the Seder. He read slowly from the Passover Haggadah, asking others about things that he was not sure of himself. Advice and questions not foreseen by the Haggadah constantly poured forth. The fortunate owners of a Haggadah followed him in their books. Tolik, as the youngest, asked the four questions: "Why is this night different from any other night . . ." I didn't have a book, but I remember that as I sat at that table I felt as if I could see the Exodus from Egypt in all its force, with all the details. As we conducted our Seder, our imagination carried us back thousands of years to the times of pharaohs and miracles, but in our souls we were living through our own Exodus, with all its tragedies and miracles, so dissimilar yet so closely bound to those ancient events.

[5] Conversation (Hebrew).

The words of the Haggadah rang out: "In every generation one ought to look upon himself as if he personally had gone out of Egypt." For us, this was not an obligation; it was our life.

But beneath the windows, several black Volgas waited while the K.G.B. agents kept a surveillance. When we left, the doors slammed, the agents sprawled in and the cars slowly trailed us. Each agent knew precisely who was his "ward."

When friends were leaving for Israel there was the same mixture of joy and sorrow, Hebrew songs inside and demonstrative surveillance outside. Sometimes, refuseniks' apartments were literally blockaded. This usually occurred during holidays, party congresses or visits of important foreign guests. The authorities preferred to see the refuseniks behind bars on those days, but it was impossible to break into a house, take an innocent man and throw him into jail. Even in Russia this required an arrest order and some kind of formal excuse. Once someone left his house, the excuse could usually be found. Therefore, when we discovered a blockade, we often preferred not to go out. Sometimes the apartment owners and their accidental guests would be "locked" in an apartment for several days, while the agents stationed themselves in cars around the corner, near the front door, in the elevator and near the apartment door. They were like vultures waiting for their prey.

I still don't know why my birthday attracted their attention, but when the guests got ready to leave after a noisy evening of wine, music and lively conversation, they discovered K.G.B. cars waiting for them at the entrance. Mattresses were placed on the floor and all those for whom it was dangerous had to stay for the night.

The morning was bleak and snowy, but the cars remained in their places. The agents had remained at their post all night, drinking vodka to warm up.

My friends lounged about the room, some read, some

wrote letters. Tolik offered to play chess with me. I didn't know much more than how to move the chess pieces; I didn't know that when he was still a child he was city champion and could now play fifteen games simultaneously with his eyes closed. In a word, he needed three moves. I remember every tiny detail and intonation of that morning. Then we said what we had been feeling for a long time: we needed each other.

We decided that as soon as my brother went to Israel, we would have him send us a joint invitation, as a family. We had no idea how difficult it would be for us to become a "legal Soviet family." In Istra, where Tolik was registered to live, the workers at Z.A.G.S.[6] told us, "You have too great an age difference." They were clearly mocking us because not only is Tolik only three years older than I, there is no Russian law which defines the permissible age difference of a prospective couple. In the Moscow suburb where I was registered with my parents, they wouldn't even speak to us. They too had probably received instructions regarding Tolik's status as a refusenik. When we started to press and demand, the clerk became furious:

"You'll never go to Israel together!"

We laughed at her words, not suspecting how true they would be.

Tolik rented a small room in a run-down, haphazardly built section of Moscow. Red brick buildings of the thirties stood side by side with other gray, gloomy hulks of the Stalin period. For some inexplicable reason, pieces of sculptured stucco were affixed to them. Nearby, ramshackle "wrecks" of wooden homes from the beginning of the century stood out. Compared to this "mongrel" architecture, Tolik's building appeared almost aristocratic. It was a two-story detached house from the middle of the nineteenth century, surrounded by a courtyard with huge snowdrifts. A small icy

[6] The bureau for registration of civil acts.

path led from the gateway to the entrance. At one time this house probably belonged to a single family; now five families lived in the top-floor apartment, and each with one room! The kitchen and toilet were communal; a bathtub was only a dream.

An ottoman which had been knocked together out of boards took up a third of Tolik's living space. A large rug—a gift from his parents—was spread on the floor; in the corner a small three-legged table was always piled high with books, papers, grammatical tables. Later, I covered this table with a red scarf that I bought in a Central Asian bazaar. Gradually I brought my portfolio of sketches, my paints and my easel over there.

Tolik went to work in the morning, but I was afraid to leave the room because of our crude angry neighbor who would yell about something or other in the kitchen for days on end. I didn't dare prepare food in there, only rarely would I heat up tea; I sat on the ottoman, studied Hebrew and avidly read books about Israel which Tolik had managed to get hold of. He called from work several times a day, to make sure that everything was all right, and when he returned we greeted each other as if we had been separated for years.

In the evening friends would come, drink tea and sit around until late at night. It was in this room that we helped my brother get ready for his trip after he received a visa. Tolik would talk to me for hours about Eretz Yisroel, and I feared that a telephone call or outside noise would interrupt his story.

His mother traveled from Istra to Moscow just to meet me. I waited for her tensely, but Tolik joked and gently convinced me that we would get along very well. The doorbell rang. I saw a small, elderly woman, all wrapped up. She looked at me intently as she took off her large scarf. In a minute we were sitting on the ottoman and drinking tea with candy that she had brought us. I was attracted by her open smile, intelligent face and pleasing, slightly hoarse voice. Mother and son were remarkably alike: they had the same sharp wit and sense of humor, the same open, generous attitude toward life.

I followed their discussion of family matters with amazement; I had not seen such frank trust between parents and children for a long time, especially in families where the children had decided to emigrate to Israel. This decision often frightened the parents, caused misunderstanding and tension and sometimes led to a familial break. Here it was entirely different; Tolik listened to his mother's advice on how to behave at work, reflected and then agreed with her.

Despite the accepted practice, refusenik Shcharansky had not yet been driven out of his job. When Tolik had first requested a "reference" for his visa request, his director, an amiable individual who valued such a talented worker, advised him to give up this idea. When Tolik didn't follow his advice, he became cold and distant and asked Tolik to leave "of his own free will," so that the "crime" would not take place under his authority. Then he threatened to write such a terrible reference that they would never allow him to go to Israel. As if the authorities really cared whether the most "exemplary" Soviet citizens left for Israel. It was difficult to dismiss Tolik because he had been assigned this job right after graduation; Tolik had the status of a "young specialist" and was required to work in this place for three years. This suited him perfectly but not his bosses. A general meeting was called to condemn citizen Shcharansky for his treachery. He had to stand in the midst of a furious crowd of co-workers, each of whom tried to outshout the other in castigating him. These "simple Soviet citizens" tried to demonstrate the fact that they never had anything in common with this traitor. One girl got so worked up that she called him a Zionist spy, an aggressor, who was going to Israel in order to murder her Arab brothers (her husband served in the army of one of the

Arab countries). This was the first time that Tolik was called a spy.

As we sat on the ottoman listening to his story, the three of us laughed at this detail. The room was warm and comfortable, and we were already well acquainted.

Ida Petrovna asked us how we planned to get out together since we did not have the same status: Tolik was a refusenik and I had not yet even submitted my documents to leave. I remember how sure we were that nothing bad could happen to us. The most important thing was that we had found each other. Now surely everything would go smoothly: finally some bureau would register our marriage, my brother would send us an invitation, we would receive permission and would go home to Israel at last. If we wanted to look for some meaning in Tolik's visa problems, we decided it was so that we could meet.

Ida Petrovna listened to us, smiled sadly and then said, "Please God, everything should come out just as you want it to. Come visit us next Saturday; Papa very much wants to see you."

We took the train to Istra. I showered Tolya with questions about his family, childhood, his life "before me." He told me that when he finished school in Donetsk and entered the Institute in Moscow, his family made many sacrifices to move to the Moscow area so that Tolya could leave his dormitory from time to time and be with them. His parents' life had not been easy. Ida Petrovna had waited five long war years for her soldier husband. They did not have children for years. When they finally had two sons, it was a real blessing.

Although both parents worked, he as a journalist on the local paper and she as an engineer, the family lived poorly, but the children grew up intelligent and full of vitality. The younger son, Natan (Anatoly), named after his great-grandfather, displayed an amazing talent in chess. If he disappeared, his mother always knew where to look for him. He could be found wherever there was a chess match. In Moscow I often noticed how Tolik was drawn to the chess problems posted on every newspaper window we passed.

They predicted a great future for him in school, and even his restless nature didn't prevent him from receiving a gold medal. His teachers at the Institute were convinced that he would have a brilliant scientific career.

At the age of seventeen, his best friends beat him up when they found out that he was a Jew. After that experience, Tolik began to consider himself a Zionist. By the third year at the Institute, he knew that he wanted to live in Israel. His Zionism became the only obstacle to his "brilliant career."

Absorbed in his recollections of the past, I traveled to Tolya's parents' home in a place called New Jerusalem after the local monastery and church; at this time of year Christian pilgrims, mostly wrinkled old ladies in black, flocked there. I felt as if I were going to visit very dear relatives. We walked past the monastery woods along a snow-strewn path. Black tree trunks protruded from huge snowdrifts. Clumps of snow fell from the bare treetops to our feet; the crows cawed. This "new" Jerusalem was so unlike our real one which we would finally get to someday. Closing our eyes, we could even imagine ourselves walking along the narrow, blindingly sunny Old Jerusalem streets, so familiar to us from postcards.

Tolya's parents' home was a gift to me. Suddenly two homes entered my homeless life at the same time—ours in Moscow and his parents' in Istra. Everything there was suffused with kindness and humor. An atmosphere of trust and warmth prevailed.

When Tolya's father saw me he lit up. "Finally the Shcharansky family will be tall." (All the Shcharanskys are short; I'm very much the opposite.)

I loved to spend time at their home. We would go there to "get warmed up" and to eat good food; we would also sit it out there when Tolik was being followed too brazenly.

One winter night, when I was looking out the window for Tolik, I suddenly heard an engine roar. I saw a black Volga slowly enter our snowy courtyard, pressing Tolya with its back fender. An hour or two later, another car just like it squeezed in the gateway and pressed against a refusenik who was coming to visit us. We couldn't understand how the cars would eventually get out. They remained under the window, so we knew that everything we would say could be overheard. We had no secrets, but we couldn't stand feeling like fish in an aquarium who were being stared at malevolently. All evening we were silent or communicated with paper and pencil.

When the K.G.B. cars tried to leave in the morning, one got stuck in the snowdrifts, thereby locking the other in the courtyard. The roar of the engines woke up the neighbors. Sleepy and in a state of aroused curiosity, they poured into the yard, trying to find out what such luxurious cars were doing there. Our pursuers became enraged; without waiting to find out what happened, we got our things together and left for Istra.

Two days later, a young policeman dropped in on us, looked at us and our guests in confusion, demanded everyone's documents and asked whose apartment it was. He kept looking at us curiously and finally couldn't contain himself:

"Who are all of you here?" he asked with the childish smirk of a conspirator.

"People," Tolik answered mockingly.

The policeman left and returned several hours later.

"I have been ordered to have you cleared out of the premises within twenty-four hours since you are not registered here. So get going," he said harshly.

In the morning, the neighbors began unceremoniously peeping in. We moved to a room in another house on the same street. In a month, the same incident was repeated. We moved six times in six months, until we landed in a small one-room apartment on the edge of Moscow. Here the K.G.B. left us in peace for a while. Because of its distance from the center of town, the apartment was relatively cheap: it cost us fifty rubles, half of Tolya's monthly wages.

After all the torments, we were delighted with the privacy of an individual apartment which had a small kitchen where we could prepare food at leisure without the unfriendly scrutiny of the neighbors. Our Hebrew group began to meet there twice a week. In a period of six months many students went away, new ones replaced them, the teacher changed, and quite often Russian words would be heard in spite of the rules. But all of us valued these lessons greatly. I put Tolya's declension tables on large colored tablets and hung them up in the kitchen. By this time I could already write some of the psalms of David in Hebrew, and we often sang them to Jewish tunes.

Tolik continued to go to work, but the situation there became more difficult and threatened to end in his dismissal. Not only would that mean the loss of our only income but, more importantly, Tolik could become one of those unemployed refuseniks with the threat of arrest and trial for "parasitism" hanging over his head.[7] Attempts to register our marriage were as fruitless as before. My brother in Israel sent us an invitation which we couldn't use. One of our friends advised us to investigate the possibility of getting married according to Jewish law. One Saturday we dropped in at the synagogue. In the enigmatic semidarkness we were met by a man to whom we delivered our request. Recognizing Tolya, he became very frightened.

"You're planning to go to Israel and you stand on the other side of the street on Saturdays! I can't help you. Anyhow, you have to be registered in the marriage bureau in order to conduct the ceremony. Try your luck in some other city."

[7] In the U.S.S.R. a person who hasn't worked for three months is considered a parasite and is liable to criminal prosecution.

His answer left us little hope, but nevertheless, the idea appealed to us more and more. After all, we were almost Israelis, and what would be more natural than going through the Jewish marriage ceremony, the only "legal" one for us? Tolik, having received Israeli citizenship, renounced his Soviet citizenship and busily wrote letters to the Supreme Soviet and to O.V.I.R.[8]

I couldn't stop thinking about the marriage *chuppah*. I went again and again to the synagogue, spoke with several people, but always saw the same fear in their eyes.

The situation seemed hopeless. I would spend entire days sitting in the little square opposite the institute where Tolik worked, and he would seize every spare minute to come out to me. We would sit in the spring sunshine, dreaming about Israel. The desire to live there was so strong, and we were so engrossed in the details of our future life in Israel, that it seemed real, and the square with its benches and pale-gray passersby became part of some prolonged, absurd dream. When Tolik finished work, we went home together; we feared separation more than anything else, perhaps because it was already evident that we would not succeed in leaving the country together. Somehow or other, one of us would receive permission first. Tolik insisted that I submit my documents; he was very fearful for me. I delayed doing it, hoping that he would receive a visa soon; then I would see him off and manage to get out myself.

It was a difficult time. On the day when Israeli children were murdered in Maalot, we joined a spontaneous protest demonstration near the Lebanese embassy. Fifty of us were met by hundreds of soldiers. We stood tensely facing them for a long time. When one of us raised the hastily written placard "Shame on the murderers!" the melee began. The

[8] As a sign of their frustrated desire to emigrate to Israel, some refuseniks have requested and officially received citizenship from the state of Israel. As a further mark of protest, Anatoly also openly renounced his Soviet citizenship. Neither act was acknowledged by Soviet authorities.

soldiers grabbed us and flung us into police vans, the Black Marias. After spending a night in the detoxifier at the Kiev Railroad Station, we decided that it was impossible to go on like this: we had to get out somehow; if not together, then individually. Tolik convinced me that if I could emigrate, it would be easier to "drag" him out from Israel; he produced a thousand reasons.

In the spring I submitted my documents for repatriation to Israel.

One day I phoned Tolik, as usual, at work. They told me that he had gone out. When I called later, he had not yet returned. I waited for him in vain the whole evening. I checked with his mother in Istra, but he hadn't called there. Not wanting to frighten her, I didn't explain anything. I spent the entire night telephoning friends and acquaintances. In the morning I found out that he had not come to work. I asked to speak to the director.

"They arrested Tolya," he said fearfully and hung up.

At the Central Police Department on Petrovka Street, a sleepy uniformed man leaned out of a small window. He listened to me, looked through some lists. "Perhaps some accident?" Sifting through the papers, he began evasively to explain something about an order given by certain "agencies" whom he could not name. I accused these anonymous "agencies" of hooliganism, and he advised me to clear out or they would "take care" of me too.

At the exit, I bumped into an acquaintance who was also looking for her refusenik husband. She had seen him being taken away when he went out to buy cigarettes. Calling around, we found out that many of our friends had been arrested. They were expecting Nixon in Moscow and probably decided to hide the "recalcitrant" Jews so that nothing would overshadow the important guest's visit.

Ida Petrovna arrived in the evening; she had sensed that something had happened. We discussed a plan of action and she left to make an inquiry with the Istra police. They told her that Tolik was under preventive arrest. That evening a lawyer friend explained to me that preventive arrests are illegal in the U.S.S.R. The following day they summoned me to the O.V.I.R.: "You can receive your exit visa."

From that moment, Ida Petrovna didn't leave me alone for a minute. We decided that I should request an extension, which was sometimes done if someone had unfinished business. I waited in the long line at O.V.I.R., and reached the office at the end of the day.

"Your visa expires on July fifth."

They gave me only two weeks for preparations instead of the usual month. I asked the clerk to extend my visa, explaining that according to the law I could use it for a year.

"What's your problem? Maybe you don't want to take advantage of your right to repatriation after all your protests and demonstrations?"

I tried to explain my situation to her, arguing on a personal level why this extension was so important to me.

"That's none of my business, write to the director," she retorted indifferently.

I wrote a statement. Depressed, Ida Petrovna and I sat in the empty O.V.I.R. waiting room for a decision. The answer came down from upstairs: my request was not granted. We didn't know what to do. The next day we tried again and again to convince the O.V.I.R. workers, but we kept receiving the same reply: either leave now without problems or the visa would expire, and I would never see it again. They said that if I did not use the visa, Tolya and I would be in for more trouble. Yielding to pressure and threats, we finally paid the money for the visa. Suddenly the clerk, who had been screaming at me a minute ago, extended her hand:

"Pleasant journey," she smiled. As I was leaving, she called after me, "I think your husband will join you soon. It's a matter of a few months."

I decided that in spite of all the threats, I would not leave if I did not see Tolik first. I steeled myself and vowed that we would have a chuppah no matter what.

A week earlier, a man at the synagogue had said that he would try to help me. He didn't know that Tolik was a refusenik, and he didn't promise anything, but for me it was a peg on which to hang my hopes. That Saturday at the synagogue he invited me to come on the following day.

Passing through a darkened entryway, I froze with surprise: my friend sat in a sunlit room, rocking rhythmically, quietly reciting prayers. A large cream-colored shawl with black stripes covered his shoulders. A thin black strap encircled his arm. For me it was like a picture from another life. From time to time, he covered his eyes with his hand and then the indistinguishable prayers became clearly pronounced words. He finished, noticed me, sat me down and began to put all these strange objects back into a handsome bag. I quietly watched him, not understanding how he could help me. Soon another man entered; tall, proud-looking, with a tightly compressed mouth, he seemed inaccessible. Clearly, I would have to tell him everything—about Israel, Tolya's refusal and my visa. He listened thoughtfully.

"No, I can't do anything for you. I can't tell the rabbi that you want to go to Israel. He will get frightened because it is dangerous for him," he explained and began asking me some additional questions.

Apparently losing interest in me, he then began speaking to my acquaintance about their own affairs. I was so distressed and full of despair that I didn't even hear when he turned to me again:

"Don't you have a photograph of your fiancé?"

I took a small picture out of my pocketbook. Suddenly he grabbed it out of my hands.

"Tolya! It's Tolya! Why didn't you say so right away? I know him; he's a remarkable young man. You're a lucky girl! We've had many long talks with him in the synagogue. He's an unusually bright boy, your Tolik!"

I burst out crying. From that moment we worked together to arrange the chuppah. Tzvi, as he was called, warned me right away that it was an extremely difficult undertaking, but that he would take it on. I trusted him completely. Every evening we would meet and he would teach me the various things I had to know before the wedding. While waiting for him on some street, I would try to guess by the expression on his face what news he was bringing. He gave me several dates when it would be possible to arrange the chuppah, but each time something was wrong. July 5 was not only the day when my visa expired, it was also the beginning of the three weeks of mourning before the Ninth of Av, a period when Jews do not perform marriages.

Finally, we set the only possible day: the fourteenth of Tammuz (July 4). I was so involved in these arrangements that I almost forgot that I was to leave soon. The only thing I requested of heaven and fate was that Tolik would be released by the designated day. Ida Petrovna helped me in all ways. We decided that we must do everything in our power and hope for a miracle.

We cleaned the apartment thoroughly and made food for the wedding. The friends and acquaintances who came to say goodbye to me asked in amazement about the strange preparations. On the evening of the third, Tzvi came with his wife to make sure that there would be ten men for a minyan. I hurriedly finished sewing my dress. Only Tolik was missing.

On the morning of the fourth I left the house to invite friends to the wedding. "Has Tolya come back already?" asked the wives and sisters of his arrested friends. They probably thought that I was crazy. I returned home slowly, praying to myself, "Please God, let Tolya be home now!" When I saw him, unkempt, exhausted, quietly conversing with his mother, I wasn't surprised. My wish had been granted.

33

We hurried to finish everything: quickly showering and shaving, Tolya ran with me to buy a ring, a white tablecloth and various other necessities.

We appeared again on Arkhipov Street. Tolik remained in the square while I crossed the street and entered into the dark, cool synagogue corridors. They were expecting me, and we completed the preparations for the chuppah. When I went out the side door, the street was empty. The setting sun illuminated the leaves on the trees, which were reflected on the pavement as spots of light and darkness. As Tolik came to meet me, I saw in his face that he, too, felt that we were experiencing a miracle.

At home everything was ready. Friends in the same un-kempt, emaciated state as Tolik were waiting for us. Tzvi supported the aged rabbi. We repeated after the rabbi the unfamiliar but cherished words. The glass was broken in memory of the Temple's destruction. The words sounded out: "If I forget thee, O Jerusalem, let my right hand lose its cunning. Let my tongue cling to my throat if I will not remember you, I shall put Jerusalem at the head of my rejoicing."

Tolik covered my face with the veil. Then the gaiety began —the group danced around us singing in Hebrew with their hands on each other's shoulders:

Soon may there be heard
In the cities of Judah
And in the streets of Jerusalem
The voice of joy and gladness,
The voice of the bridegroom and the voice of the bride.

We sat nearby and listened to Tzvi. He gave examples from the Bible of miracles which occur when you want them desperately. The guests rejoiced in spite of everything, even the black Volgas which were surrounding the house. Tolya and I saw only each other and quietly tried to catch up on everything that happened during our long separation. We tried to understand what had just happened to us and what awaited us the next morning, but we couldn't. There wasn't time for a long farewell or for talk about the future. We thought that Tolik would join me in a few months, but now we had to face separation. We knew that it would surely be longer and harder than the fifteen days which we had just survived with such difficulty.

"Write me a little, but often, about everything," he said. "I want to see your life there clearly, so that we won't be separated for a second."

It was still long before dawn when we left the house. At the airport the customs officer rummaged through my suitcase for a long time, turned the Jewish marriage contract over in his hands and with a sign of incomprehension, stuffed it back in again. Tolik stood by silently. I kept begging him to go home and rest up. I went up the steps and looked back for the last time; friends were waving to me and shouting farewell. Tolik stood a little to the side and silently stared at me. I whispered, "Come soon," as if he were already far away and we missed each other terribly.

An airplane took me first to Vienna and then to Ben-Gurion Airport. Warmed by the Israeli sun, gradually accustoming myself to the blinding light which revealed distant, wonderful landscapes, I finally felt at home. I felt calmer, more at ease. I was certain that within three months Tolya and I would be reunited.

Anatoly's Letters to Avital

My dear Natulya!

The first week of our separation has passed—that means one week less. This week was fast-moving yet tedious, anxious yet joyful. Now I feel such weariness that I don't seem to have the energy to make it home. After two stormy months, a lull has set in. . . . By the way, I'm beginning to "lament" and this doesn't completely suit my mood. I'm tired, but at peace and for days on end somehow idiotically happy. I constantly feel that you and I did something beautiful which they can never take away from us.

I don't mean the chuppah itself, nor anything concrete, but simply our mutual feeling. I still don't have the strength to analyze and think things out, but there doesn't seem to be any need for it anymore.

My dear, I write you a postcard every day and wait impatiently for news from you. . . . I want to see vividly how you live, what you see, what you think. I want to picture your meeting with Misha, and the group, your arrival in Tiberias, and Jerusalem.

After a whole series of postcards and letters, I haven't written anything for several days—I'm still waiting for some word from Vienna. But nothing has come, and this saddens me. I am constantly living on treasured memories, but I don't want our present life to be tied only to them and not to new prospects. I joyfully and jealously think how much every day means to you now, how quickly you will become immersed in that sunny, noisy, tense and so confusing world which we here call "Artzenu," our land. I don't want to miss out on these significant days of your life—why yours?—our life, and therefore, with great impatience, wait for the day when your letters start to come.

TRANSMITTED VIA STERN

August 6, 1974

My dear Natulya, how beautiful you are. Yesterday, I received your pictures, your letter and a letter from Jane and Jerry.[1] Really, what would we do without such Jews?

Yesterday made it a month since you left. I remember when seven months passed after November 13, you had said, "This is already a very long time." But how little it is compared to one month of separation! I miss you terribly. At the same time I am glad you succeeded in breaking away from this dark life into the bright sunlight. This alone represents a great victory for us. Of course we shall soon be together. In September I plan to take decisive steps to attract attention to our situation—keep this in mind.

August 20, 1974

. . . With your departure, time has changed completely. You have a whole new absorbing life, but I am half with you and half in the same rhythm, in the same old situation. One half

[1] Jane and Jerry Stern, American friends who are discussed at greater length in the section entitled "Expectation."

37

drags the other after it, and that other half bursts the shell and breaks out of this banality. Every day is like a road marker; I strike against each marker with my whole body, knock it down and move on to the next. That's how I perceive time now.

My dear Natulya, I want you to understand me: now, more than ever, I'm happy you are no longer living this depressing kind of life. Despite all that has happened to me, everything is immobile, and you can fall into despair, grow dull, and rot alive from this endless vortex. You offer me another life and I avidly grasp it.

Don't take the last reply from O.V.I.R. too much to heart, okay? Everything can change at any moment. And please don't think that I am simply sitting and waiting for the weather to change. Everything is more complicated now than before.

I am trying to use the means which is most effective at the given moment.

Natulya, my dear, do you remember that I often said (and believed) that the days spent here are not wasted, that this is a unique experience? I don't think so anymore. Each day here is another stolen from us together. How I didn't appreciate time when we were together! It's a shame to think of how much time was lost, how much wasted on minutiae.

It is now six months since you left (and since our chuppah, Natulya, I congratulate you). Although I remember the days when we were together down to the minute, this half year is somehow one big jumble.

"Jacob worked seven years for Rachel but in his eyes they were like a few days because of his love for her." [Genesis 29:20] You see, I continue to read the Bible and see our life through it.

My beloved, my little sunshine, don't grieve and don't feel

lonely on the Sabbath. Do everything that Jewish women do on that day, and I shall say the Friday night kiddush over the wine as if we were greeting the Sabbath together. . . . Tov? ["Good" in Hebrew.]

December 1974

Natulya, my beloved! I'm writing to you from the telegraph office. Two curious characters in hats are circling around me like sharks before an attack. And although I am not deprived of their company for a minute, I am alone now as never before. I haven't received anything from you; I am gradually losing not only the details, but the whole picture of your life; this is terrible and sad. I am counting very heavily on our conversation tomorrow.

I have a thousand things to do now. I'm tired, but live in the hope of relaxing soon with you. I embrace you warmly, I love you, I love you. Regards to everyone.

Tolya

March 15, 1975

My dear, my beloved, how much longer will fate try us?

I'm sure you understand my mood. I have to think, decide and act in dramatic circumstances, full of confusion and uncertainty. But it is, of course, easier for me than for others. After all, I have you. Because of you my life has definition, such depth, such refined perception and a feeling of fullness that I would not exchange it with anyone.

My dear, I beg you again and again, take care of yourself, do not allow yourself to grieve deeply, don't weep. You are living now for both of us, live calmly, fully and deeply, and when I come, you will share it with me.

Soon it will be Passover. Do you remember last Passover? Since then, you, Avital Sharon,[2] crossed through Sinai, re-

2 Sharon was the original form of the name Shcharansky.

ceived the Torah and arrived in Jerusalem. I congratulate you, my dear *ishti*.[3] Although I am still in Egypt, we know that it's not for long.

March 20, 1975

Shalom, my dear. I haven't received a letter from you in a week, but I hope something will arrive before Passover. For those of us wandering over the Sinai, these are difficult days, but I have a basis for inner calm and optimism—you.

I, like many others, am helped by the conscious or, more often, unconscious feeling of historical optimism, a connection with Eretz Yisroel, which your teacher explained so well. This shouldn't sound like blasphemy, but for me this exists through you: you have turned this link into life itself for me.

. . . We read the Torah at Volodya Shakhnovsky a few weeks behind the regular schedule. Now, during Passover, we are reading about the Exodus. I don't want to blaspheme and insist that it's more natural, but still it worked out very well; the dramatic events of our own Exodus and the celebration of Passover came at the same time.

April 8, 1975

After a long break, I have returned to reading regularly. I have read two good books in English, *The Source* and *Indestructible Jews*, outstanding historical studies about our nation's path, its role and function in the world, the reasons for its survival. Perhaps these will help me in a small way to keep up with you.

I had an interesting encounter recently. I was traveling on the train from Istra, leafing through my four-language dictionary, when suddenly an old man sitting across from me asked in Hebrew with an excellent accent, "Is that a Hebrew dictionary?" We talked for a while in Hebrew; although he

3 Hebrew: wife.

spoke so much better than I, he was pleased to find a Hebrew-speaking companion. He told me he had a large Hebrew library at home and had studied Hebrew literature for many years, having perfected his knowledge of the language by listening to the Voice of Israel broadcasts. Yet he was afraid to consider any contact with the aliyah movement. When I told him who I was, he glanced around fearfully and sat as if on hot coals. Funny? A man walks around lighting his way with a match when there is a blazing bonfire next to him. But if you think of how long and under what conditions he has carried this lighted match, and that our first Hebrew teachers learned from such old men, then you can't cease being amazed at the ways of our survival. . . .

Spring 1975

Whatever we might have said to ourselves and others, the arrest of Mark and Boris [4] and everything that followed it, initiated a rather long and difficult period from which we are now finally emerging. After their arrest, I spent a lot of time talking about them with foreign journalists and lawyers and influential congressmen. This produced some results: practically no meeting between Americans and Russians in Moscow takes place without the case of Mark and Boris being discussed.

Now they are in transit, which is the worst part. Boris is being sent to the Krasnoyarsk Region and Marik to Chita. As soon as I hear from them—around the second half of June —I'll go to visit them.

June 30, 1975, 1 A.M.

. . . Right now it seems to me that when I finally arrive in Eretz Yisroel I'll lie on the sand near the sea next to you, and we'll stay there for a month or more, until I finally calm

[4] Mark Nashpitz and Boris Tsitlyonok were arrested in February 1975 and exiled to Siberia for five years.

down. Only then will I be able to live a normal human life. Sometime we'll remember the past with amazement and think, "Did all of that really happen to us?"

September 18, 1975

Shalom, my dear. The Israeli weightlifters have been in Moscow for several days. A lot of people met them, but I couldn't since I was very busy with Natanchik's case.[5] I was finally free yesterday evening and went to the Luzhniki Sports Complex. The situation was entirely different from that at the Universiad in 1973.[6] We rooted for "our" weightlifter as much as we could. It was difficult for him to compete with professionals—he is a clothes cutter from Tel-Aviv who practices only once a week. Still he didn't do badly. Then he and the other Israelis came out to us and we chatted with them for two hours in Hebrew—I really don't know where the words came from. On Sunday, I'll probably go with them to the woods to observe Succot. Our life is such that one day we meet with Israeli scientists and the next with weight-lifters.

Last night I even dreamed that you came with some team to Moscow for a competition. Of course, we were together all the time, then suddenly we realized that you were late for the game (I don't even know which). You didn't want to go, but I said, "You mustn't let your team down." We hailed a taxi and raced over—and then I woke up.

The day before yesterday, I sent you a "business" letter concerning your trip to the States. I hope you will receive it. Let Misha read it over. The people whom I mention are my friends and can help make your trip most effective.

---

[5] Natan Malkin was then standing trial for evading army service.
[6] At the international university competition in 1973, in which an Israeli basketball team participated, fights broke out when police attempted to prevent Moscow Jews from entering despite the fact that they had tickets.

My dear Natulya, my beloved,

I am writing you this letter, postmarked from the distant city of Chita, almost at the other end of the U.S.S.R. I just sent you a congratulatory telegram—I don't know whether it will reach you: it caused a big commotion. Right away I had to give up the idea of writing it in Hebrew, but it wasn't clear whether it would get to you in Russian. When I think that I can't be with you on your twenty-fifth birthday, I want to cry. I spent the last five days with Marik in Tupik. It really is a *tupik.*[7] It took five hours for Marik's aunt Musya and me to fly there from Chita on a small plane. Tupik is a regional center, but in fact it is a small town (eight hundred people) in the taiga, inhabited mainly by hunters and those who serve them, teachers, doctors, etc.

Life there is, of course, very rough. Even now, at the beginning of November, the temperature in the daytime is −15 or −20 degrees centigrade and at night −30. There are no water pipes; in the morning we dislodged a piece of ice from a barrel, and placed it in buckets on the stove. Marik learned how to stoke the stove deftly—the whole process from splitting the wood to heating up the hut took him no more than thirty minutes. I, too, learned this art by the end of my stay in Tupik. For me those were five days of rest, but five days are not five years!

Now I am leaving Musya and going to Borya. The shortage of tickets and hotel rooms makes the trip very tiring. But we'll be able to rest in the Eretz. I only hope to find Borya in as good shape as Marik.

December 2, 1975

Everyone was delighted with your large photograph, but my mother took it to Istra and won't give it up. She says that

---

[7] Tupik, here the name of a city, also means dead end in Russian.

it decorates the apartment; so please send another one. Although maybe you shouldn't send one. Oh, how it's time for me to be there already. It is no longer a question of hope or faith, but simply my way of life: waiting for a visa, not even a visa, but simply a chance to meet you. When I was with Marik in Tupik and then Borya in that disgusting Eniseisk, I imagined very clearly how we could manage in either place if I were exiled and you could come to me there. How much fuller that life would be than life without you in Moscow. Did we make a mistake? No, no, no. Destiny is letting us understand who we are and why we were given to each other.

Winter 1976

My sunshine, I have imagined our reunion and our life together in Eretz down to the smallest detail so many times that it seems as if we were already living together on our land. Since Sasha got his visa,[8] everyone is waiting for mine to come through. Two or three times a day various people ask in amazement, "You still don't have permission?" Everyone is certain that it is literally a matter of weeks or days. Now Vitaly Rubin is leaving; the two of us represented the interests of the "Zionists" in the group observing the carrying out of the Helsinki Accords. And again everyone tells me, "You're next." I try not to think about it and not to "sit on the suitcases," or else I could go crazy.

July 1976

Natulya, my dear beloved. It is already two years. It's hard to believe. Not only because I remember clearly every day that we spent together, but also because you are with me all the time. Can you imagine how you help me with your letters? Even your silence helps, simply because you exist and you are waiting. People feel sorry for us, but in my opinion,

8 Sasha is Alexander Lunts, a refusenik who waited three years before receiving his visa in 1976. Shcharansky lived with him before his departure.

fate (or God) has been very generous to give us each other.

I am writing this letter in the apartment of Mother's friend —do you remember we were there once? Now A.V. has moved for a month to Istra and I took advantage of this to set myself up here. . . . After several days of being lazy, I'm enjoying the quiet and the fresh air (the Botanical Garden is next door). I even have a television, although there is nothing worth watching; I have to compensate with Voice of America. For four days the Voice and other stations have been broadcasting the news about our boys' mission to Uganda. What an anniversary gift. My mood is excellent. . . .

1976

Your soups have really helped me out; now it's easy to eat quickly. Yesterday Lida dined with me and was delighted with the wonderful way you've devised to help me. The American boots you sent from New York were a real help in prison. Because of the stuffy, heavy air there I am still coughing, but it is passing.

In a few hours I am going to the synagogue. I don't like to, they literally tear me to pieces there; I whirl around for two hours like a hamster on a spinning wheel, but people still get insulted that I don't give them enough time.

I gave the Gerbers the portfolio of a painter whom I visited recently. He and his family (wife and daughter with two small children) want very much to go to Israel, but he would rather die than leave his pictures here. He also doesn't want to sell them to foreigners. He wants to bring all of them to Israel, and to have them become the property of some museum there. Since there are many—around 150—it is difficult to help him. Until it's clear whether or not he can leave with them, he wants to maintain good relations with the authorities and continue his work as a member of the Union of Artists. In the meantime, we shouldn't attract attention to his name.[9]

9 This artist has been in Israel since 1978.

Consult with A.L. on how he can be helped, and I shall look for some way here. The series of 150 pictures is mainly about old Jewish Odessa.

Yesterday I visited Andrey Dmitrievich Sakharov—he and our Helsinki group talked with an editor from *Time* who is now visiting Moscow. His last question concerned the Jews who are going to other places than Israel. There is a lot of talk about this now in Israel and here. Of course, it is unfortunate, but I fear that what the authorities plan to do about it (or are already) is more unfortunate and could undermine Jewish emigration. . . .

Regards to Mishka, Benjamin, Ilana, Hannah (how does she feel, when is she due to give birth?), Tzvi and all our friends.

I kiss you warmly, my beloved Avital.

Your husband Natan

December 30, 1976

Natanchik Malkin, apparently, is being transferred "to chemistry."[10] If you don't know what this is, ask Sasha [Lunts] to explain. In his case it's probably good. At any rate, he will be able to eat normally.

Recently I sent you an invitation letter. You should get a questionnaire from the Finnish embassy and fill it out.[11] Do this (you will probably receive a refusal) quickly and tell me, Natulya, *tov*?

The fate of many people in need of help depends on me; if I described some of the people and their situations, nobody would believe me. For many who are devastated by separation from their families, time destroys the strongest ties. I am happy that for us it is the opposite. (I think I already wrote you about that, but this thought comes to me so often that it's no surprise that I repeat it.)

[10] Forced labor building new industrial enterprises in the provinces.
[11] A request by Avital to visit Anatoly in the U.S.S.R. received no official response.

October 19, 1976

When I spoke to you, your sorrow and your hardship reinforced my exhaustion so thoroughly that everything seemed unbearable. My dear one, how can I calm you, how can I take away your tiredness, your pain? My dear, my beloved Natulenka. Better that I should tell you how I have been living recently. The day before we talked to each other—that was Thursday—I gave a report on our operation in Entebbe, Uganda. It was given at Rubin's seminar in Feliks Kandel's apartment. A very good man, Arkady Mai, now leads this seminar. About fifty people came and I was completely surprised. I didn't expect to give such an interesting report; I could see from people's faces that it held their attention, not so much because of what I said as the topic itself. After all, everyone knew everything and how it ended, except for some basic details. I gathered all the material that had appeared in the Western press. The correspondents I know brought me copies of articles, a book, a radio interview transcript and other information about these Palestinian terrorists in other operations. I talked for three and a half hours instead of one and a half. All kinds of people were there from professors to fifteen-year-old kids. The whole time there was such silence and such suspense on their faces. When I finished there was such joy, as if everyone had just relived it all. Mark Zakharovich ran to kiss me, acting as if I were the very pilot who had landed the first airplane in Entebbe. This really was one of those moments when I felt that I had done a *mitzvah*, even though it was very easy, and pleasant work. My good mood continued . . . and then it was Simchas Torah when you commanded me to rejoice, and I tried to rejoice, but it was somehow very difficult. But then Enid and Connie arrived unexpectedly and we were together in the synagogue. Enid told me a little about the Sabbath you spent with them in Jerusalem and

I felt that you were with me and it was good.

I am speaking now in the Slepaks' back room, do you remember we once studied Hebrew here. . . .

My friends from Odessa are arriving soon. They had some problems (searches) and want some advice. Then there are some people from a small town who are afraid of being seen, but very much want Jewish books and information on Israel. I am supposed to meet them and give them some things. Then Enid and Connie are leaving, and I shall go today to the municipal O.V.I.R., perhaps today I can conclude my discussions on the municipal level. In a week there's an appointment at the All-Union O.V.I.R.—I'll go there with our applications. I found out that in the U.S. Senator Leahy had already gone to the Soviet embassy with a request that your application to visit me be granted.

I would like to talk to you in a leisurely way for the whole tape, to sit and simply talk, not about anything specific, and that's all. It's nice to think that in a few days you'll be able to listen and to send me another tape. Only please, as fast as possible.

Today is October 19; in twenty-five days it will be our third anniversary. My God! How I would love to be with you, and perhaps I shall be with you yet. I think, if they'll let me go, they'll give me five days, and I won't ask for any more, it's enough. And three days—it's also enough. Only it should be soon.

Enid asked how to help us. Yes, many people love us. . . .

Why are we so sad, my dear Natulenka? I want to tell you something cheerful, joyful. I remember how we went to that apartment to study Hebrew and you couldn't say a word, and how you tricked me before that, saying you knew so much in order to be in the same group with me, do you remember?

And now you speak Hebrew so well I am embarrassed. Tomorrow I'm going again to Shakhnovsky to start studying with him again. It's very important to study Hebrew; when I arrive, you'll be my translator. Here I am the translator for everyone and there you'll be mine.

An amusing incident occurred recently.

The tails were following me—the surveillance was intense and crude, with threats—in general it was "jolly," you know that they even traveled with me in taxis and paid half without arguing, they were so afraid to let me out of their sight, and even then two of their cars were driving behind me.

In the midst of all this I receive a telegram—that is, Mama receives it in Istra. They are trying to put an urgent call through from Montreal. I can't get there, simply no time. With difficulty I transfer the call from Istra to the Central Telegraph building. I think, "Well, it's urgent, I must appear. But I'm so busy!" I appear with my tails, they give me the call and some people tell me, "An entire school is listening to you in Montreal, would you like to say something to us?" I mumble a few sentences, am confused, then they say to me: "We would like you to greet the Sabbath together with us now." One girl tells something about herself, reads a prayer and lights candles. A boy says the blessing over the wine and bread, the kids sing something and dance. I am listening to all this and my tails are standing next to me and the place is full of people.

Then they say to me, "Now we are all together, the whole school is listening to you, let's get up, Natan, and we'll sing 'Hatikvah'!" Do you understand? And I get up, well, what can I do, and begin quietly to sing "Hatikvah." All the people in the telegraph office look at me as if I am an idiot. . . . Okay, we shall laugh some more sometime.

I often have the feeling that I want to sit down and write my memoirs—I feel so old, but fortunately this desire quickly passes.

It would be better to write humorous stories instead of memoirs. There is so much absurdity in this life.

I beg you not to despair, your mood is very important to me. Get this tape soon and send me an answer and let us soon be together.

Expectation

A gray pickup truck drove away from the noisy airport. Benjamin is sitting next to me. Ilana and little Hannale are waiting for us in Tiberias. We haven't seen each other since they left Moscow two years ago. Everything about Benjamin amazes me—his tan, the shorts he's wearing, his ability to get along in this blinding world.

"This is a back road, full of construction sites, orange groves, gas stations. You are lucky, Natashka; since you have returned home, you get to see all sides of the country at once. No, maybe it's better to sleep a bit, I can see you are tired, the light has blinded you. . . ."

But I couldn't sleep. The last few agitated days and sleepless nights, parting. . . . The lights of Tel-Aviv from the airplane window and tears of joy. The meeting, the noisy crowd, the palms on the searingly sunny plaza. I was feverish from excitement. Outside—wasteland, golden seaside sands, and suddenly, round green hills with flocks of sheep. Then the white, simple little homes of Afula, colorful signs, the soft, wooded hills of Galilee. When Mount Tabor came into view, its vineyard-covered slopes and green fields, shining with drops of water splashed from long rows of whirling sprinklers, I closed my eyes in exhaustion:

My God, I am home, home! This is my land, all this splendor is mine, mine! How long it took me to get here!

Even in childhood, when I didn't even know this country existed, I always felt out of place in Russia, as if I were among foreigners.

My father fled from Poland to Russia to escape from the Nazis. He fought in the Soviet Army and married after the war. At the beginning of the fifties, he, like many others from that wave of refugees, was exiled to Siberia with his young wife and two small children. I grew up in a small town on the last railroad station of the Siberian railroad. As a child the most common words in my vocabulary were "exile," "camp," "camp prisoner," "escape." . . .

My parents were dedicated Communists and did not mention our Jewishness to us; they tried their hardest to ignore it. Choosing to forget their roots, they gradually seemed to forget their very selves. Both served the authorities—Father in the camp supply system, Mother as a prosecuting attorney —and both were quick to defend the very regime which had exiled them to Siberia. They willingly overlooked the obvious and believed in all kinds of falsehoods.

Probably in the depth of their souls they felt some kind of dissonance but, never confronting it, they immersed themselves deeper in their work, became harsher, more irritable and insular. They took out their dissatisfaction on us, their children. Our home situation was oppressive; almost every day ended in conflict. When we were still very young, my brother and I would run away from home and spend whole days in the swamp.

When my brother grew up, he would disappear into the taiga for weeks in order to get away from them. Once, when he was fifteen, he went away and didn't return. We found out that he had gone to Mother's relatives in Moscow, whom we sometimes visited in the summer and whom we both loved. Grandma, dark-haired, tall, swarthy, in her wide flowered skirt, seemed to be an enchantress—all the happiest childhood experiences, the tasty, spicy smells of a Jewish kitchen, interesting walks were associated with her. How I wanted to run away with my brother! But he was grown up —tall and strong—while I was still small and had to resign myself to remaining in Siberia, in a home that was even more oppressive without his protection.

When, after lengthy exertions, my parents succeeded in returning to Moscow in the sixties, Grandma had already died. The oppressive atmosphere of our Siberian home settled into my beloved grandmother's apartment. My brother, a university student, lived independently and rarely visited us. Home life became more and more unbearable. When I finished school, I began studying painting at an art institute and went to live with my brother.

Together we "wandered," renting "corners" and rooms, "roaming" from place to place around Moscow. I lived in a semiconscious state. The city seemed hostile, I felt superfluous everywhere, as if I had mistakenly wandered into some alien world. Somewhere, without fail, there must be a place for me—which I would recognize immediately. And in Israel I recognized it—my world, my land—from the first glance. . . .

My reverie was interrupted when someone touched my shoulder. We had stopped at a small kiosk. Our silent Israeli driver, looking at me kindly, offered me a bottle containing a brown liquid:

"It's hot, refresh yourself a little."

Something cold and sweet tingled in my mouth, thousands of tiny needles stung my throat and eyes, even crept up to my forehead. My first encounter with Coca-Cola amused everyone.

We drove down to Tiberias. Below, the Sea of Galilee sparkled like a blue mirror. The Golan Heights formed a wall behind it. In the valley beneath us, tinted all possible shades of green, nestled the small white homes of kibbutzim and moshavim. The descent, a turn and we are riding in shady streets with trees like delicate bouquets; another turn and I see Ilana with her little daughter on the terrace of a new, light-colored home.

The huge window in my friends' apartment was like a frame for a beautiful picture—the sea, the sun-steeped golden mountains, the overgrown gardens. . . . I couldn't tear my eyes away. Everyone began talking to me, explaining, asking. . . . I tried to answer, but the world was so different and so were they, and I seemed to be not myself. I felt as if I didn't understand their Russian.

The setting sun tinted the view to the color of smelted gold, then silvered it. The new, blinding world was submerged in dusk. The lights went on and I recognized the familiar Turkmen carpet draped over a low table to serve as a couch, the teapot, Oriental bowls and sweets, the same intimate atmosphere I had shared with these dear friends two years ago in Moscow. The shock gradually passed, I reacquired the gift of speech. Making ourselves comfortable, we sat drinking tea until the morning. I told about friends, relatives, about everyone who remained there, and all the time I felt Tolik's absence. This feeling was so strong I can remember that several times I wanted to turn to him to affirm or add to my story.

My Hebrew course, the ulpan, was scheduled to begin in Jerusalem in several weeks. In the meantime, I could relax, recover my strength, lie in the sun on the shores of the Sea of Galilee. Tiberias was for me a small-scale model of Israel. I had time to find my way, so that later, when I would go out into the large, unfamiliar world, I wouldn't get lost. Each day was full of events and new impressions; at times my mind seemed simply unable to withstand the pressure of all this information. In the evenings, after the traditional tea on the ottoman, when the house was engulfed in quiet, and the locusts chirped in the sultry, aromatic side streets of Tiberias, I wrote to Tolik. Shades of color, smells, overheard fragments of sentences, chance meetings—all went into these letters so that Tolik could experience each new Israeli day together with me.

When I returned, as usual, weighed down by impressions from my regular sortie into town, Ilana greeted me with relief:

"At last you're here! Some Americans are looking for you. They went to the ulpan in Jerusalem, the Jewish Agency, everywhere; they combed the whole country and miraculously found us. They're coming in the afternoon. They have news from Tolik!"

I became excited:

"Maybe something happened? They've given him a visa and these people are coming to tell me about it! Who are they? How am I going to talk to them? After all, none of us knows a word of English, and my brother, who could help us, is far away on an archaeological expedition!"

Jerry and Jane Stern came in smiling, with the mysterious look of people knowing something very important. They hugged me, handed me Tolik's picture and letter. My first letter from Tolik! With the help of a neighbor's son whose English was scarcely better than ours, but primarily through the mimicry and gestures of Tolik's friends, I learned that these people had just spent several days with him. As tourists in Moscow they had met a group of Jewish refuseniks and had fallen in love with my vivacious and open Tolik.

I wanted to ask them about everything, every detail was important to me. Dear Jane and Jerry tried so hard with smiles and intonations to convey to me their admiration for Tolik! Finding out from him that he had just said goodbye to his wife and hearing our saga, they volunteered to be his emissary. Arriving in Israel in the heat of a July hamsin, they made their way across the whole country to Tiberias in order to give me a "fresh greeting" from him. My ignorance of the language didn't hinder me. I seemed to understand everything. I had the feeling that these people were relatives, that Tolya and I had found friends to whom I could turn with any request without embarrassment. Time proved how correct this first impression was; since then, Jane and Jerry have always given us support.

My studies at Ulpan Etzion in Jerusalem began. I was placed in a room with a girl from Greece. Although we barely understood each other, we were glad because the absence of a common language stimulated study; it forced us to practice our little bit of Hebrew constantly. Each morning we got together in class: a businessman from the States, a couple from South Africa, some young men from Argentina, a nice young boy from England, an old woman from Morocco and myself. The lessons were intensive but relaxed. Each student had the opportunity to tell about himself and his country and, in turn, to question others. At these times a marvelous feeling was created: before our eyes pictures of people's lives from all ends of the earth, various experiences and varied fates whirled by.

Together we discovered the same truth: the fate of Jews everywhere is alike. It is amazing how such different people understood each other so well when the subject was anti-Semitism, the continuous feeling of homelessness and the instability of temporary well-being. All of us, old and young, without fail, had at some time either gone into hiding or fled to save our lives. The elderly American, who looked so well off, had by a miracle escaped from Nazi Germany, wandered for a long time in Europe without the right to settle anyplace until he finally made his way to America. The English boy's parents had fled from pogroms in Russia. The old woman from Morocco remembered how she had hidden for weeks, afraid to appear on the street where a savage mob screamed "Death to the Jews!" The Argentinians had fled from a real hot spot. They told about relatives and friends who had disappeared without a trace. The couple from South Africa had also fled, feeling that there was no future for Jews in their country. I recalled my father's flight. He was the only survivor of the Holocaust from his large Hassidic family. And my own life, too, was in fact a flight.

And now, finally, we had stopped running, we were home. This diverse family had gathered here from the ends of the earth. We could talk with each other and recount what had happened to us over the two thousand years of separation and wanderings.

After classes I hurried to the ulpan office. They would greet me either with a joyful smile—that meant a letter had come from Tolik—or with a hasty greeting which signified no letters. If no letter arrived for several days in a row, I felt empty; the waiting became unbearable. I couldn't study and went out to "breathe in Jerusalem." Long aimless walks about town restored my strength. Jerusalem was very kind to me. In those first days, people on the streets smiled at me with particular warmth. If I had a problem, they gladly helped. Something about me immediately told them that I was a newcomer. *"Olah chadashah?"* ("A new immigrant?") asked bus drivers, kiosk owners, postmen . . . *"Yihiyeh tov"* ("Everything will be okay"), they encouraged me with a smile. And I thought that if these fugitives from all the corners of the earth, who had already survived four wars here, were so sure that *yihiyeh tov*, then it really would be okay, it couldn't be otherwise.

The blinding whiteness of the city surrounded me. The ancient terraces of the Judean hills, overgrown with olive groves and vineyards, were covered with scattered white stones. These stones seemed like flocks of white sheep grazing on the slopes, descending into the innumerable wadis, and there in the green of meadows and gardens they were resting. How naturally the city, built from the same white Jerusalem marble, fit into this pastoral landscape—as if these animated stones had gathered together, evened off their rough edges and behold, a house was built. Sometimes, along the slope of a hill, a burdened-down donkey trotted slowly by. Or a Bedouin shepherd drove a flock of sheep.

Biblical pictures came to mind: Abraham left his tents in Hebron not long ago; he came here, to Mount Moriah, with his only son Isaac, prepared for anything but fervently praying that the horrible sacrifice would be avoided. Right near here, Jacob slept, putting a smooth warm white stone under his head, and in his dream he saw a "ladder reaching into the heavens." Miracles occurred—it seemed so easy for me to "remember" the history of two, three, four thousand years of antiquity and to experience it as if I were a participant. The scanty biblical pages acquired flesh, aroma and color.

I spent the evenings with Tolik, looking over his letters and pictures. I wrote to him about everything that my eyes saw. I tried with all my might to picture his life. Where is he living? What is he eating? We are still enjoying a warm, sunny autumn, but there it is already snowy winter. What is he wearing? He doesn't have warm shoes and no doubt he will freeze in his overcoat! My God, why can't we in one burst drag him out of there and bring him here? He would look so natural in that street crowd, no one would even guess that he is an *oleh chadash*!

Letters did not arrive regularly. Sometimes they simply disappeared; other times, in despair after weeks of waiting, I would suddenly receive a whole bundle. The postmarks showed various dates, sometimes even different months. We joked, "The censor went on vacation." But how dearly we paid for his frequent vacations!

Around wintertime, having gotten used to the work rhythms of our censor, Tolik sent me "messengers" and "emissaries" with letters, notes and stories about him. Almost every week, I would travel to the airport to meet some family or other. After much questioning, I gradually got a picture of his life.

"He lives, like before, in friends' homes, always moving from place to place. He is constantly busy, burdened with work: he helps everyone, is totally reliable. He barely sleeps,

57

eats when he can, his entire possessions are the portfolio in which he keeps your letters and pictures, a toothbrush and a change of warm underclothes in case of a preventive arrest."

My five-month ulpan class was drawing to a close. It was time to think about arranging my life. Tolik wanted me to finish studying. There were several possibilities: I could go to the Bezalel Art School, or to various seminars or courses. I had only to choose. But I didn't hurry. Every morning I arose with new hope that today, this very day I would receive a telegram with the priceless word "visa." I would meet Tolik and together we would decide. . . . I had the feeling that without him I couldn't really lead a normal life. After all, he also had an abnormal life! We were caught in limbo. Our life consisted essentially of waiting and in waiting there is no movement. Simply a stop, an entr'acte or interlude between two lives—the one which we had had together and the one which would be.

I began thinking more frequently about how I could help him. I told our story to various visitors in Israel from Europe and America. Many promised to help and then I began to feel that I wasn't simply waiting, that it was in my power to change something. Our faithful friends Jane and Jerry Stern did not forget us; when the gaps in correspondence became especially painful, we would correspond through them. In the fall of 1974, Jerry wrote to Congressman Ed Koch, who turned to Dobrynin with a request to let Tolik leave. Having verified our marriage contract, the ketubah, at the rabbi's office, I sent Tolik a new invitation, attaching proof of marriage to it.

By this time I was already carrying on a rather large correspondence with various people in Europe and America. Some saw Tolik, others asked how they could help, and others didn't even ask but acted, asked their congressmen to intervene or wrote to the Soviet embassies. . . . All of this instilled hope. I felt I was participating more in Tolik's life. My life seemed split in half: only one half lived now in Israel, the other half lived with Tolya in a foreign land, in depression.

I started to work part time in an immigrant absorption center, so that I could devote all the rest of my time to efforts on behalf of Tolik. Three months had long since passed. Our separation had dragged on for almost a year. New hopes would flare up and quickly be extinguished. . . .

I was again living with Ilana and Benjamin, who had moved from Tiberias to Jerusalem. Together we considered all kinds of possible ways of helping Tolik. My brother Michael, then serving in the army in Sinai, would come on his leaves and help us cope with the English-language correspondence which had piled up during the week. From the stories of newly arrived refuseniks, I understood what a hard life Tolik was leading, how much he was working. This work had long since lost any connection with his work in the Institute, where he used to go every day when we were together. They had somehow managed to throw him out, and in order to earn his bread and not be brought to trial for parasitism, Tolik had to give lessons in English, physics and mathematics. His open nature, his reliability, his bright head made him the center of attraction for many Jews who ran into difficulty in the perilous path toward repatriation. Someone is not given a reference from work; Tolik tells him how he should demand it and stay within the law. Another faces trial for parasitism. I saw this man in Israel; he rapturously praised Tolik. "How did he help you?" I asked him. He became impassioned recounting how he was threatened with trial, exile. . . . "That's what would have happened if it weren't for Tolik. He traveled a thousand kilometers to come to us, took charge of the situation, demonstrating his magnificent knowledge of jurisprudence, helped me write letters to all the authorities, went with me to meet petty officials, finally the danger retreated and look, I'm in Israel. And only thanks to him!"

In Odessa someone's wife was dying; Soviet doctors did not know how to cure her illness. In Israel, they knew how to treat it, but the family had been receiving refusals for several years. Hearing about this, Tolik went to Odessa. I met this family in Israel; they were eternally grateful to Tolik and felt that only thanks to his help did they finally get out. (Indeed, by then it was already too late, the disease had gone too far and the young woman died almost immediately after her arrival.) My Tolik was helping everyone, but where could I find someone who could help him? I thought when I listened to these stories.

The beginning of 1975 was a difficult time for Moscow Jews. On February 24, our close friends Marik Nashpitz and Boris Tsitlyonok were arrested during a demonstration. Refuseniks for four years, they had taken part with Tolik in the very first demonstrations, and had often been in our "nomadic" home.

We all loved Borya Tsitlyonok, gentle, calm, with large warm eyes, a pale, bearded face. His friends tenderly called him Boryunya. His father, mother and brother had left for Israel several years ago. For some reason, Borya was denied a visa. His unexplained refusal was incomprehensible to everyone: he had never been connected to the notorious "secrecy" and in general presented no "value" to the state since he was a simple factory worker.

His homeless life and longing for his family undermined his health; he developed a stomach ulcer and I often noticed how waves of pain passed over his sad face. We would meet him at Hebrew lessons, "farewells" or at friends', where he could always be found, silent, friendly, at the record player. Half closing his eyes, he sat listening to Israeli folk songs.

His friend, the young doctor, Marik Nashpitz, was the

complete opposite of Boryunya—enterprising, restless. . . .
Life as a refusenik was very difficult for an active person like
him. Unlike Boryunya, he knew the reason for his refusal
and felt himself a real hostage.

When he was still a child, his father went abroad on some
mission and didn't return. Later, he found out that his
father had settled in Israel. Marik's connection with Israel
was long-standing and deep. In his house one could hear the
best Hebrew songs and learn interesting details about life
in Israel. When he requested an exit visa, he was told that
he could leave only when his fugitive father returned to the
U.S.S.R. Not wishing to remain a hostage for life, Marik
decided to go out every day, alone, to demonstrate in front
of the Supreme Soviet building. He went there every morning, knowing that he would spend the rest of the day in the
police station, but that in Jerusalem his father would appear
every morning at the Wailing Wall with a placard appealing
for support of his son. This went on for almost a week. Marik
grew thin, dark with an overgrown beard, and finally collapsed with a bad cold. . . . Later, whenever I saw him, I
pictured the sun-drenched white plaza with the wall and the
solitary figure of the father, waiting for his son.

In 1974, Marik's mother received permission and left for
Israel, but they reaffirmed Marik's refusal and he remained
alone. Some time later two K.G.B. agents came to his house,
glanced around, quickly made themselves comfortable and
without any introduction proposed that he work for them.
According to them, he should go, like before, to demonstrations, remain "himself," but be ready to be of any service to
the K.G.B. For this they promised him a visa. Marik became
infuriated and drove them away, cursing them roundly. The
following day he phoned the correspondent from the London *Times*, who published the whole story. Marik's arrest
a month and a half later was probably an act of personal
revenge by the K.G.B.

The excuse was the demonstration of February 24. Two months earlier, on the anniversary of the Leningrad Trial,[1] a group of refuseniks lodged a complaint with the Presidium of the Supreme Soviet, demanding visas and amnesty for the prisoners. After waiting two months for a reply, they decided to demonstrate. They chose the empty plaza next to the Lenin Library, a place without cars or people, so that they couldn't be accused of "disturbing public order." Tolik was then living with Lunts, a well-known leader of the aliyah movement, whose apartment gradually turned into a haven for those needing a bed, advice, help.

Tolik set off alone on the morning of the demonstration. Although a few succeeded in reaching the spot, almost all the participants of the planned demonstration were seized along the way. Tolik, approaching the library, managed to unfurl his placard for a second, and they immediately pounced on him and dragged him away. Everyone met in a small room in the library where each one was brought under guard. They held them there for an hour without any explanation; then as usual, they put them in a bus and sent them to the detoxifier. At nighttime, they began to release them. They waited for one another on the sidewalk. Seven were missing. They soon found out that five of the missing ones had been arrested for fifteen days, but Nashpitz and Tsitlyonok had been taken away somewhere in a Black Maria. Someone suggested that they would be brought to trial, but no one wanted to believe it.

The trial took place in a month. The two were accused of "disturbing public order." They didn't allow anyone into this "open" trial. The witnesses for the defense were turned away.

In the month between the arrest and the trial, Tolik worked day and night. He wrote letters to everyone, informing, explaining, asking for help. A group of California law-

[1] The trial of a group of Jews accused of hijacking a plane to leave the Soviet Union.

yers, then visiting Moscow, tried unsuccessfully to attend the trial. They went with Tolik to every division of the Supreme Court from the lowest to the very highest—all in vain. . . . They were never permitted to enter.

The harsh sentence—five years of exile to Siberia—was completely unexpected. The K.G.B. attitude toward the Jewish aliyah movement had clearly shifted. Apparently some decisions had been taken up above. For several years there hadn't been any trials of activists in Moscow; the authorities disobeyed their own law on the sly. Preventive arrests for fifteen days, detoxifiers, threats, disconnected telephones, unmotivated refusals were already customary, as if there were a defined limit of injustice and illegality which had not yet been transgressed. All the refuseniks who actively fought for their right to emigrate first studied Soviet law thoroughly. Knowing that thousands of eyes were following their every step, they acted exclusively within the legal framework, and Western public opinion and publicity provided them with relative security. But the farther they were from Moscow, the less the refuseniks felt protected by the law; there not even the appearance of legality was maintained: the K.G.B. used unjustified trials, psychiatric hospitals, exile and imprisonment to frighten those who had not yet submitted documents to leave for Israel.

In Moscow, overflowing with foreigners, correspondents and embassies, knowledge of the law had, up to this time, been good protection. Some Moscow activists were even considered great legal specialists and helped advise others. Tolik was one of them. It was his style—legality and publicity. He tried to help his friends, distant and close, everyone and anyone who needed it. This demonstration, too, had been entirely "legal." They had carefully chosen this spot since the only basis for detention in this case could be "disturbing public order." Nevertheless, they accused Marik and Borya of just that. Neither publicity nor blatant illegality stopped the K.G.B.; the authorities had gone on the offensive. . . .

The mood was oppressive. Many decided to behave quietly after this trial. It was no longer possible to rely on the law. It was a terrible time. Tolik was among the few who kept their presence of mind. He felt that precisely in such a situation it was important to remain oneself, to do one's own work, striving for truth and justice in a country of lies and unchecked lawlessness.

Irene and Sydney Manekofsky, friends from Washington who had met him in Moscow, received a letter from him in the beginning of April in which he noted:

"You know, of course, about the dramatic circumstances of our present life. We are not giving in, and we are trying to look ahead optimistically. Your support is a very serious basis for this optimism."

Even foreign visitors felt this oppressive atmosphere among Moscow Jews. The Sternbergs and the Danielses, two American families, visited the Soviet Union in June. They called me when they arrived in Jerusalem:

"We have greetings and pictures for you from Tolya."

I dashed over to their hotel, the sooner to see and hear. Lately letters had not been arriving at all. Still carrying a strong impression of their trip, they recalled:

"Right away we felt that it is difficult to breathe there. Our first day we went to the Slepaks'. With difficulty we found their place. In the completely dark entryway, a man was sitting, pretending to read a newspaper—in complete darkness! When we visited Slepak again the following evening, the house was surrounded on all sides by the same kind of people wearing identical outfits, who circled in groups.

"Wherever we went with our new friends, we would see the same faces behind us, the same black cars, slowly trailing us along the sidewalks.

"One evening we sat alone in our hotel room and spoke

about the courage people like Tolik, Lunts and Slepak have to be able to live in such a situation without losing their spirit.

"Suddenly the door opened. A man entered the room without knocking. He carefully, slowly looked us over and calmly left. We felt very ill at ease that evening. In three days we left Russia.

"We all felt miserable. Although we had flown away, our friends remained with all this—the tailing, the threats. We had had enough of this after a few days, and they had been living like that for years. When the airplane rose into the air, a burden fell from us, which had been oppressing us all those days.

"Suddenly everyone sighed at once, even began singing from joy that we were free, that we were flying away from this terrible place."

It was evident, however, that they did not feel real relief; they were too shaken up by what they had seen, they had taken the fate of their new friends who were left there too much to heart. June Daniels was always on the verge of tears when telling me about Tolik:

"What can we do for Tolya? Tell us and we'll do it!"

What could I tell them? If I only knew the formula! We sat together for a long time trying to think of something. For the first time it occurred to us that I should go to America in order to appeal to the Soviet authorities through official people there. After all, Israel has no official relations with the Soviet Union, not even an embassy in front of which, at least, one could protest, go on a hunger strike. My new friends were sure that in America I would find understanding and support, and who knows, maybe then it would be possible to drag Tolik out of there. On my way home from the hotel, I thought that, in spite of everything, fate had been extraordinarily generous in sending us such friends.

* * *

I received very sad news from Tolik. They had arrested his friend Natan Malkin. For several years Tolik had been watching over this very young, delicate, sensitive boy who amazed all of us with his iron will. Tolik wrote me a lot about Natanchik, as he fondly called him. The boy's strained relationship with his parents reminded me of my childhood and youth. I wasn't surprised to find out that his mother and father did everything in their power so that their son, a third-year university student, should receive a refusal to his visa request. He was immediately dismissed from the university and right away sent an army call-up notice. Natan knew from friends' experience that army service would prevent his getting permission to leave; after all, even participation in the army wind orchestra or in a building battalion could become the reason for many years of refusal because of so-called secrecy. Moreover, for a long time he had considered himself a citizen of Israel and wanted to serve in the Israeli forces, but definitely not in the Soviet Army. He thought everything over, weighed it and wrote to the Minister of Defense. He didn't receive an answer, but the notices kept arriving. Still hoping for a reply from the ministry, Natanchik temporarily moved in with friends to avoid receiving notices. His parents, knowing well how this would imperil their son, reported his new address to the police. Natanchik was arrested.

In the three months between arrest and trial, Tolik devoted all his time and energy to Natanchik. He constantly informed Western correspondents in Moscow and his numerous friends in Europe and America about the course of events, explaining what a terrible precedent Natan's sentencing could set, especially now, in the atmosphere of fear and uncertainty following the trial of Nashpitz and Tsitlyonok. He felt that with this trial the authorities were warning thousands of young Jews aged seventeen to thirty, particularly students. He even prepared a special document demonstrating that in Malkin's case, the army call-up was used as punishment for his desire to emigrate to Israel.

Nothing helped. On August 26, Malkin was sentenced to three years in a labor camp.[2] Tolik was correct: Malkin's case was only a link in a carefully worked out program aimed at scaring young Jews all over Russia. Right after Natanchik, they condemned Yakov Vinarov in Kiev on the same article, and Silnitsky in Krasnodar. They took Vladimir Feldman into the army by force, and started cases against Levitas in Kiev and Kovner in Gorky.

How much more difficult it was becoming for Tolik to "breathe." Sometimes it seemed to me that a noose was tightening around him and his friends. And these milestones that he mentioned in his letter—each day was like another milestone he had to overcome—and then the next day and the next marker. An endless fence was dividing our lives. Lord, give him strength! To hold out, to remain himself! I didn't need to make an appeal for that. At times his strength seemed fantastic to me. His smile and his humor, even in the worst situation, never left him for a minute. I seemed to see his free, calm stance and his ironic smile when he wrote me about his detention and conversations with the K.G.B. He was detained because he and his friends planned to travel to Babi Yar, that ravine near Kiev where on September 29, 1941, the Nazis shot 33,000 Kiev Jews. Another 100,000 Jews were shot there later that fall. For twenty years the Jews tried to get permission to build a monument to the victims.[3] At the end of the 1960s, it became a tradition to travel to that spot on that day and read the Kaddish, the memorial prayer for the dead. And each time the authorities tried to stop them, and it often ended in arrests. . . .

At this time Tolik was living with his friends the Slepaks.

---

[2] Malkin recently arrived in Israel, having served out his sentence.
[3] The authorities put up a memorial at the beginning of the seventies, but the Jews are not mentioned at all in the inscription.

Tolik wrote:

Some notes from my recent detention: For four hours a
K.G.B.nik conversed with me (or rather tried to converse);
I think he is supposed to or has already replaced Sazonov [4]
(they also have their "change of generations"). In compari-
son to Sazonov, the conversation took place in a spirit of
"détente"; instead of direct threats—a very careful remark
with which he could compromise me, for example, when I
receive a visa. He threw out endless propositions in an attempt to set up an "informal" situation. He alluded to the
difficulty of coming to an understanding with me because
I tell every "private" conversation to my English-speaking
friends.

Suddenly he would change his tone and say sharply: "I
warn you, if even one word gets out of this room, you'll be
sorry!"

"What do you mean? I fear your organization too much
to have any secrets in common with you. I'll tell everything,
down to the last word, to everyone who wants to hear it."

After several warnings followed by my repeated assurances
that I feared them too much for that, he suddenly said, "All
right, have it your way, but listen, what I'm going to tell you
now, please, not a word."

"No, better then not to say it, I'm going to tell everyone
everything all the same."

It was a real vaudeville. Ten to fifteen minutes later he
said: "No, I want to tell you and I will tell you, but not a
word to anyone else."

And I to him:

"No, better not say it, I'll tell everything anyhow, I'll go
straight to the first telephone booth. . . ."

So I didn't find out the big K.G.B. secret. But he still
didn't stop trying to share some worthless secret: he informed
me that the spy Abel is Jewish and asked:

[4] The K.G.B. expert on Jewish matters.

"Please, not a word about this!"

I repeated again that I would certainly tell everyone.

"What, you're really going to tell everyone that Abel is a Jew?"

"No, of course not. I am going to say that in my opinion, Abel is a Latvian, but for some reason the K.G.B. insists that Abel is a Jew."

His attempt to find a mutual language ended there. He warned me that I was being detained in Moscow because I was like a wanted criminal(!). I complained to him about the brazenness of the tails. He denied their existence, but when I walked out onto the street at eleven o'clock at night, my tails (including the most vicious one, who had threatened to beat me up a day earlier) were all kindness and good will. When, just as I had promised, I went up to the first telephone booth to call correspondents, they offered me a handful of two-kopek pieces. They then rode with me in a taxi (although two of their cars followed behind). After an unsuccessful attempt to make them get out, I told them:

"You'll pay."

They didn't agree.

"Half and half."

The next day I intentionally rode everywhere in taxis, paying for only half of the trip. The second half was paid out of special envelopes. Now I know the real meaning of "détente."

Tolik kept in very close touch with the accredited Western correspondents in Moscow. His excellent English and his facile ability to sum up and analyze a situation made him irreplaceable. He gradually became the "voice" of the aliyah movement. If something happened to someone, Tolik informed the West about it; he prepared a survey on the situation of Jews in Russia. He didn't sleep nights, traveled to various cities gathering information on new refuseniks, on illegal obstacles. With tourists, his presence was indispensable. In the summer and fall of 1975, there were many Western visitors in Moscow who were interested in the situation of the Jews and met with refuseniks. Representative Robert Drinan visited in early August. He and Tolik became friendly when Tolik acted as his guide, translator and adviser for several days. From that time on, Drinan took a very active personal interest in Tolik's fate. He wrote Tolik:

"Dear Anatoly! I can't express my enormous gratitude to you for the hospitality you showed me in Moscow. I am much obliged to you personally for the success of my trip. Be assured of my active efforts to help you emigrate to Israel."

Robert Drinan has kept his word and remains one of my husband's most dedicated friends and defenders.

The much publicized meeting between a group of Jews and ten American senators also took place that summer; Tolik served as translator. Later, that meeting became one of the points in the accusation against him. Senator Leahy brought him a letter from the Sterns, and Tolik gave him a letter for me (letters no longer reached us by ordinary mail). Tolik also met with Congressmen Yates and Fenwick, who, in a later meeting with Brezhnev, inquired about Shcharansky's fate and were personally assured of a speedy reply. They haven't received an answer yet.

At the time, all these meetings, acquaintances and promises encouraged us greatly. Our separation became a misunderstanding that could be resolved, especially if such important, concerned people decided to intervene on our behalf. My brother, my friends with whom I continued to live, and I seriously considered the Sternbergs' and Danielses' suggestion that I travel to America to try and help Tolik from there. When I wrote about my plans, they willingly offered to help me. The Sterns, too, gladly joined in their efforts.

The trip posed various problems: my ignorance of English and lack of funds, and all kinds of technical complications. They contacted the National Conference on Soviet Jewry in

New York, who took it upon themselves to organize and finance my trip. It was decided that my brother Michael would travel with me as translator and aide in such a big, unfamiliar country. Right away I felt better.

My departure was set for December. At the last minute we changed plans and went to Canada first instead of New York. The previous summer I had met three women from Montreal—Barbara, Elaine and Wendy—who were visiting Israel. They had accidentally met my brother, then serving in the army in the Sinai. He found out that they had been interested in Tolik's fate for a long time and had been doing a lot for us, without our even knowing about it! We began corresponding, and when they heard about our plans they immediately invited us to Canada.

We flew into Montreal on November 22. We had prepared carefully for the trip: Tolik's biography, important details of his studies and a description of his M.A. thesis, his refusal, were all translated into English. Our fate seemed to depend on this trip: we mustn't forget anything, must apply all our energies. The feeling of responsibility was huge. Before the trip I was bursting with all kinds of different emotions, apprehensions. . . .

I desperately did not want to leave Israel, even for this one month. I had just begun to take root in this land. I felt as if I had returned to my real, previously unknown self. I had found wonderful friends with whom I shared so much. I gradually became familiar with our holidays—so beautiful and deep. My childhood and youth had been so distant from all this. The second Hanukah in my life was approaching. I wanted to make up for lost time. Little by little, I learned to light the Sabbath candles, to read the Bible in Hebrew. My friends Rabbi Tzvi and his wife Hannah taught me the simplest things, which are known to almost all Jews except for us "refugees" from the Soviet Union. I felt good in Jerusalem. I hoped that my wanderings had finally come to an end. Tolik would come, we would build our home here, we would have children, they would go to school. Each morning I would make them sandwiches and put them in snack bags. Israel contained the fulfillment of all my desires. Here I had achieved clarity of thought. I wanted to live and live here, without leaving for a minute.

"What's the matter? Why are you so upset?" asked Tolik in a telephone conversation before my trip—one of the occasions when my efforts to converse with him met with success. "After all, you can't spoil anything, you can only help. Don't be upset. Remember our friends—Marik, Borya, Natanchik —and it will be easier for you to speak. I'm not worried about your meetings with people. Just be yourself. Everything will be fine."

It was freezing cold in Canada. I hadn't seen such snow-drifts for a long time; I had even forgotten about their existence. The landscape reminded me of Siberia. We had become completely unaccustomed to the cold, to the low, overhanging clouds. We froze and felt a tightening in the chest because days went by without the sun appearing at all. But our Canadian friends received us with special warmth. Barbara hosted us in her own home. She, her husband and her five children took such good care of us that we didn't need to worry about anything. On the day of our arrival, Elaine, Wendy and a few others got together to work out a program of activities and to divide responsibilities.

When we met with journalists, they questioned us about Tolik and about Jewish matters in general in Russia. We spent evenings in homes and synagogues where all kinds of Jews gathered to hear about the incomprehensible life of their brethren in the U.S.S.R., no Jewish schools, no yeshivas, no legal possibility of studying Hebrew. We told about ourselves and our friends, and these simple stories upset them, caused some to cry.

On one of these evenings I attempted to put a call through

to Tolik. I thought I might have better luck breaking through to him from Canada than from Israel. Since we were invited to appear at a school that evening we rang him up from there. We phoned for a long time; the group waited around hopefully. The telephone operator in Moscow said that Tolik had come and gone away. I didn't believe her. Fifteen minutes later we called again; another operator said that he hadn't come at all. We made one more attempt; they said they had no request for such a call. It was a graphic demonstration to the schoolchildren who were listening. We were bombarded with questions.

We rushed around for a week without stopping once: interview after interview, constantly meeting new people, constantly repeating the same story—ours and our friends'. My brother and I were completely worn out. Yet, setting out for each new appearance, we felt an influx of strength. Perhaps just this particular meeting would turn out to be decisive. Perhaps we would meet some people who would know how to help us, or someone very intelligent would give us an idea, a "strategy" to help us drag Tolik out!

In the evenings we rushed to Barbara's home to light the Hanukah candles. The whole family gathered together, the children sang the traditional songs. Israel was here, with us. Then again meetings, interviews, acquaintances.

We spent so much time parting with our hospitable friends, hurrying to complete unfinished business, to finish saying the unsaid, that we missed our flight from Montreal to New York. Only first-class tickets were left for the next flight. We knew that Jerry Stern was waiting for us at the airport in New York, but we didn't have enough money to pay the difference. The situation was unpleasant. Suddenly a man and his wife approached us and without questions or explanations paid for our tickets, saying that they had seen us in Montreal, knew that we were not just "out for a ride" and were happy to help us even in such a little way.

Jerry Stern met us at Kennedy. We drove through the New York night to his home to eat and rest.

"Here you are in America, child," he smiled and quietly began telling us how he had appealed to three senators to help us. They had turned to Dobrynin, but hadn't received any reply. The brightly lit, somehow unnaturally empty streets drifted past outside the car window.

We spent two days in New York making plans, met with various people and constantly felt the guardianship of the Sterns. Jerry and Jane worried about whether we were comfortable in our hotel, had eaten enough and were warmly dressed. They did everything quietly, in a familial way.

The tempo of our journey through America was crazy: today we are in New York speaking before newspapermen; after dinner we have a meeting with the city mayoral candidates to tell them our story. Toward evening we are falling off our feet. Tomorrow we go to Chicago, then out West, and everywhere we can expect meetings and appearances; the days are scheduled down to the minutes.

The Danielses met us in Des Moines. We were again with a family which enveloped us in loving care. People gathered in the Daniels home in the evening. Few people from Des Moines had been in the Soviet Union; we were the first Russian Jews this community had met. It was very important to tell them about what is going on in the U.S.S.R. Learning that one of the guests was planning to travel to Russia, we bought warm boots and asked him to give them to Tolik. Later Tolik wrote me that these boots served him very well during a fifteen-day sentence.

In Louisiana we warmed ourselves up a bit; the palms and sunny skies reminded us how much we already longed for Israel. In Baton Rouge we visited the friendly home of Donna and Hans Sternberg and met members of the Jewish community in the synagogue. When we left, the rabbi of the synagogue presented me with a small copy of a Torah scroll and promised to pray for Tolik.

We returned to New York completely exhausted, but with the feeling that many people would remember Tolik and wouldn't let him "disappear." In almost every place were people who had either met Tolik personally or heard of him. Through hearing about our and our friends' experiences, many began to understand what is happening in Russia, and some actively joined our efforts to help Tolik.

After listening to the story of our travels, Jerry said, "Not bad, but what about Washington?"

We shrugged our shoulders.

"I think we must go there," he said. "First of all, you have Tolik's letter asking you to meet with his friends, Congressmen Drinan, Yates and others. I also know a senator whom I'll ask to help. Of course, everything depends on luck, but it's worth trying. We don't have any choice. We'll appeal to everyone. It's decided. I'll take two days' vacation, and we'll go to Washington."

The meeting with Senator Frank Church of Idaho was set for the evening. In the morning we were already walking down the endless corridors of the Senate and Congress buildings, knocking at office doors.

Senator Patrick Leahy of Vermont cordially invited us to come in, heard us out and told us that he would be happy to act as a courier during his trip to Moscow. He took a letter for Tolik and brought one back from him to me.

Congressman Joshua Eilberg and his wife, Gladys, received us very warmly. They had become friendly with Tolik during their trip to Moscow, corresponded with him and were among the first who tried to help him.

Another corridor. Jerry recognizes someone, stops, points to me, explaining something, the latter nods, asks us to drop in. It turns out that Jerry knows this senator only from his pictures in the newspapers. He promised to arrange some meetings for us the following day.

Congressman Drinan gave us a hearty and noisy welcome. Lively, very energetic, with a nice, delicate face, he immediately began to tell me how he had seen Tolik and spent several days with him. Noticing how attentively I listened, he understood that he was giving me an opportunity to get a sense of Tolik, and with loving detail he spoke slowly about my husband. He disappeared for several minutes and returned with a group of his colleagues whom he had told about us. They all came to make my acquaintance. It was decided to arrange a press conference with Drinan for the next day.

In the evening we met Senator Church and his wife. They knew about Tolik and had been trying for more than a year to help him. They were very understanding and promised to double their efforts.

By the looks on Jerry's and Jane's satisfied faces, I could see that we were succeeding.

In general these people treated us very sympathetically and humanely. They were not dealing with some impersonal political problem, but trying to help people in trouble.

Two more days in New York and then home! The Sternbergs and Danielses flew in to say goodbye to us. Everyone thought that the trip was a success. We hoped that the help of so many people would quickly bring results. We slept soundly in the airplane. The emotional voice of the TWA pilot awakened us:

"We are approaching Israel. We are approaching the Holy Land."

I couldn't hold back my tears. Michael buried his face in the window. The familiar strip of surf near Tel Aviv, the clear blue, almost lilac, sky. The air in our country smelled of orange blossoms, pines and cedars growing alongside the road which gently led us up into the mountains.

"You could eat this air in teaspoons for dessert," joked

Michael. We silently rode up to Jerusalem. The city opened up like a book. Beyond each mountain a new one, a snowy white page with etched groves of olive trees, with steps of stony terraces.

Dusk. The street lights went on. A huge yellow moon sailed over Jerusalem.

"Dear Jerry and Jane," wrote Tolik to the Sterns, "Today I received Avital's letter sent from the U.S.A. on the day after your trip to Washington. She writes about meetings with congressmen and senators and about your role in organizing these meetings. She also writes that you took good care of her and Misha during their visit. Dear friends, I can't thank you because you asked me not to. But I want you to know how deeply I feel the reality of Jerry's words that we are one family. I dream that Avital and I can host you and your children in our home in Jerusalem, and I hope that it will be very soon."

We indeed hoped that it would be very soon. The beginning of 1976 was a time of hope. After our trip to America, rumors began to spread that Tolik would soon receive permission to leave. These rumors were intensified after Lunts's departure. A refusenik for many years, Lunts was a close friend in whose home Tolik had been living recently. No one knew who started these rumors nor what they were based on, but everyone both in Tolik's circle of Moscow friends and here in Jerusalem spoke of Tolik as if he were already packing his suitcases. I remember phoning an acquaintance, a distant relative of Tolik's, late one evening from work.

"Do you know that Tolik has received a visa?" she asked.

"When? When is he leaving and how did you find out about this?"

"Yesterday at some friends', I heard it."

I couldn't speak. Tolik received a visa! He's coming! I

must run home quickly, tell everyone. I have to do something! But how come acquaintances know it and I know nothing? Maybe a telegram is waiting at home? No, Ilana would call at once. Maybe it's all false? Again rumors. I quietly tried to take myself in hand.

I tried to call Tolik for several days in a row and finally succeeded. His first words made it clear that there was no visa. Thank God I was already prepared for this. He told me, incidentally, that he had been a member of a five-man delegation of refuseniks who had been received by Albert Ivanov, the expert on the Jewish problem for the Central Committee of the Communist Party. "State interests are higher than the rights of the individual," declared Ivanov, but he promised that the refuseniks' cases would be reviewed very soon.

That was not all. That was less than two weeks ago, and Tolik had received a postcard to appear at the O.V.I.R. office, he had just received it. There was some ground for hoping that this time there finally would be a visa. Otherwise, why would they call him? We tried, in any case, to convince each other that it wasn't worth it to hope too much. Yet the conversation always returned to the same point:

"If it is a visa, then I won't use my month for preparations. I only need five days. Even three."

"Soon we'll be celebrating Purim. What if you send a telegram but it doesn't reach me in time and I can't meet you?"

"It'll be fine. Just imagine, it's Purim, you're all sitting down for a festive dinner and suddenly I come in!"

"Could you find us?" and I quickly begin to explain where the San Simon District is located, how to find our home.

"You don't need to go on," laughed Tolik. "I know Jerusalem like my five fingers."

The O.V.I.R. office reconfirmed Tolik's refusal. We were back at the starting point.

"Today we are celebrating Purim," he wrote, "and despite everything, I think we should not complain about our *purim.*" [5]

In Moscow on May 12, 1976, eleven people announced the formation of a Helsinki Group. Soviet papers had written a surprising amount about the conference and the signing of the Helsinki Accords in August 1975. One of the clauses of the accords stipulated that the signatories would ease emigration and would improve conditions for contact between people of different countries. This was precisely what the Jews on their way to Israel needed. Many decided that a new period was starting and that it would be easier to emigrate, but in a few months it became clear that the Soviet authorities were not planning to honor the accords which they had signed. The number of refuseniks rose sharply in the winter of 1975. Often, without even stating the reasons for refusal, the officials would add cynically:

"You have been refused in accordance with the letter and spirit of the Helsinki Accords."

The aim of the Helsinki Group was to monitor the observance of these accords and to help in carrying them out. The group gathered information and published documents about the various violations of human rights in the U.S.S.R.

Many of these problems concerned emigration, reunification of families, freedom of religion. These materials were sent regularly to the Soviet government, the Soviet press and the governments of all the countries which had ratified the accords. They were never published in the Soviet press and no reply was ever received from the government. V. Rubin and A. Shcharansky were the two activists from the Jewish movement in this group. Later, when Rubin received a visa and left for Israel, Slepak replaced him. Several documents published by this group were devoted entirely to the violation of the Helsinki Accords with respect to those who

5 *Purim* means "lots" in Hebrew.

wanted to leave Russia; a large part of the material was based on the experience of the Jewish emigration.

Tolik's work for the group placed a new, very heavy burden on him. He collected data, took an active part in compiling reports, etc. New arrivals in Israel told me that he completely neglected himself, worked eighteen hours a day, didn't have time to have a proper meal and never slept enough. One of the participants in the Helsinki Group was Elena Bonner, wife of Andrey Sakharov, whose house Tolik visited. I began to hear rumors about the special sympathy which Sakharov showed to Tolik. I deeply respected this man, who always found the courage and strength to help everyone, to intervene on behalf of everyone, and I was happy with their friendship.

The summer marked two years of separation. I tried to sum up: for two years my life is expectation. I am not studying. I am working at temporary, day-to-day work. I don't have a home. Perhaps I made a mistake? If I were to build my life here solidly, with the future in mind, perhaps Tolik would arrive more quickly? It suddenly seemed to me that our life was in the balance and that his serious life, which was so important for so many people, outweighed my unsettled life here—and therefore I couldn't draw him here. All this was nothing more than a hope of finding some kind of "mystical strategy," an attempt to outwit fate. I decided to begin seriously to build my life, to appear as if I were waiting for Tolik, not every day, but every week or month.

Tolik, Ilana and Benjamin, Michael and I considered all the possibilities and decided that I should first finish studying and acquire a profession. Since there was nothing suitable for me in Jerusalem at the time, I enrolled in a painting course for art teachers in Beersheba. Leaving Jerusalem with difficulty, I plunged into my studies. The distances in our country are short, but each city, each region, is a world of its own: landscape, climate, even type of people, the mood on the street, can all be different. Beersheba, a new, dynamic city in the midst of the Negev, is a big contrast to Jerusalem. But it had its own charm—the dry, hot days and cold, transparent desert nights, when huge stars appeared near, in the amazingly black sky; the camels casually strolling on the automobile-filled streets, the unique opportunity to wander into the endless desert at any moment.

But still I yearned for Jerusalem. Fortunately, I returned home on Thursday evening. Friday and Saturday were free to spend with friends, in long walks through the Jerusalem hills and with letters from Tolik which managed to arrive one way or another during my absence. Reading his letters, I felt his pain; these two years seemed monstrous. If I could only see him for a short time. Even prisoners are allowed one visit every half year, and we, "free" people, can't see each other for even a few days.

Perhaps I could receive a visitor's visa and travel to Russia. How could this be arranged? When I wrote about it to Tolik he answered that we shouldn't count on anything but we ought to try. I contacted the Finnish embassy in Tel-Aviv, which represented Soviet interests in Israel, and the consul's answer encouraged me. I received and filled out the necessary applications from them. Tolik received instructions from the O.V.I.R. and sent me an invitation by letter. Everything was solid, "legal"; I began to have real hopes. I suddenly believed that I would arrive there, that Tolik and I would appeal to the authorities and perhaps would finally receive a tangible response. Even if they sent me a refusal, perhaps my inquiry would remind the authorities one more time of our problem and they would finally let Tolik leave. I sent a copy of the documents which I submitted to the embassy to Senator Leahy so that he could intercede for us in the Soviet embassy in Washington. Tolik also received a copy of the documents and brought them to O.V.I.R.

We started waiting. No permission came. Nor did a refusal. My inquiry produced no answer whatsoever. Three months later, I wrote all our friends in America that I hadn't received an answer to my request for a meeting, and I asked for their help. On November 7, *The New York Times* published a declaration about Tolik and me, on the initiative of Jerry Stern. We began to receive hundreds of letters from *Times* readers. Many sent us copies of their letters to the Soviet embassy, to the Moscow O.V.I.R., to Brezhnev. And there were some unexpected letters:

An Arab woman from Lebanon wrote, "I would like to see all Soviet Jews as emigrants in our neighboring country, Israel. As a Lebanese Maronite I know very well what suffering is. . . . Please accept my modest donation—five dollars for the publication of this declaration."

One letter shook me up—a few lines written in a terrible scrawl: "Again, it's you damned Jews! I'm sorry that Hitler didn't finish you all off!" There was no return address and it was impossible to read the signature.

A republication of this declaration, timed for the day of President Carter's inauguration, appeared in the *Washington Post* on January 20, Tolik's birthday. This coincidence gladdened and encouraged us.

Meanwhile, in Moscow a real war began between the refuseniks and the K.G.B. A year had passed since the signing of the Helsinki Accords. During this year almost none of the refuseniks had left, new ones had joined the ranks; people were waiting for years without work, between "heaven and earth." On September 18, twelve people, driven to desperation, sent a registered letter to the Supreme Soviet, inquiring why they had been refused and when they would receive visas. They waited for a month, but the legally established time for an answer passed without any response. Early in the morning on October 19, they arrived at the reception room of the Supreme Soviet with a letter stating that since their written inquiries were not answered, they would like to be received and heard. No one would take their letter or talk to them. In the evening they were put on a bus and let out on the outskirts of Moscow.

The following morning they again went to the reception room with the same letter and again waited there all day. Half an hour before the end of the workday, the policemen closed all the blinds; simultaneously, two doors opened and cursing and screaming "damned yids," about forty nonuniformed men burst into the room. They swooped down on the refuseniks, tied their hands, dragged them out into the courtyard, pushed them into a bus and piled onto the bus themselves. Moscow was left behind. They drove for a long time in the darkness through the forest. Foul curses filled the bus. They shouted in Chernobylsky's face:

"Today you'll turn up your toes!"

They tried to extinguish a cigarette on Slepak's forehead. Many Jews had their clothe torn. The bus stopped in the woods, people were thrown out onto the snow and the beating began. It lasted for approximately half an hour. They trampled people with their feet. They pushed Joseph Ahs into a ditch, holding his head down under the water. They broke Zakhar Tesker's nose, Polishchuk's ribs.

Everyone was left bloodied, with torn clothing. The bus with the "civil guard"[6] left. The Jews somehow made their way out of the woods, got rides from passing cars to the nearest railroad station and from there went to the Slepaks' in Moscow.

Tolik phoned the usual correspondents and that night an improvised press conference took place in Slepak's home. When the correspondents left, they began considering their next move. Those who had been beaten decided to go to the M.V.D. (Interior Ministry) the following morning to complain and demand an investigation.

Tolik, Slepak and Dina Beilin thought that they shouldn't go alone; they needed to get additional people. They spent

[6] K.G.B. agents often disguise themselves as members of the voluntary civil guard.

the night going to the various refuseniks' homes, telling them what had happened.

The following morning fifty-two people appeared at the M.V.D. reception room. The authorities were visibly disturbed. In the West, the morning newspapers had already reported the beatings. The Interior Minister, Shchelokhov, promised to receive them, but only one by one. The Jews did not agree, insisted that he receive Shcharansky, Slepak and Chernobylsky as representatives of everyone. He agreed to receive them, and said that they would not discuss visas. With regard to the beating: "The M.V.D. can not guarantee the safety of Jews who go to the reception room of the Supreme Soviet." Then he suddenly began to tell them that even he, the minister, has a friend who is Jewish. He lives in Odessa, and would you believe it, he has no desire whatsoever to go to Israel!

The conversation ended on this note. It sounded like a bad joke or blatant mockery. Those waiting outside heard their emissaries' tale and, pinning yellow Stars of David on their chests, walked through the center of town to the waiting room of the Central Committee of the Communist Party. They submitted a complaint and declared that they would wait for an answer. As usual, no one talked to them.

As evening approached, the atmosphere became tenser. Shortly before closing time, a policeman came in and stated that they had one minute to disperse. From the window they could see that about two hundred police officers had been brought in and had cordoned off every access to the waiting room. Everyone, especially those who had been beaten the previous evening, was terrified. But to leave would mean to yield to the gangster tactics of the K.G.B. which could then become common practice. They decided to stay.

"Joseph Ahs, who had almost drowned in the icy ditch the previous evening, stood," one of the participants later told me, "such a quiet, quiet man, the father of two small children. And I could see how he was hesitating, hesitating. Finally he said:

" 'Well, that's it! I don't want to stay, but we have to stay.' "

Many of those who came to support the beaten ones also hesitated. But it was clear that if they left, the remaining ones would be crushed. Everyone remained. The doors were closed, and then the police officers burst into the room. The Jews were prepared for the worst. They were thrown into buses, conveyed to the detoxifier and given fifteen-day sentences. Some were released but arrested in the next two days, either when they left their house or in the subway. It seemed as if the usual scenario was being played out.

But this time everything was more serious. The man who told me about it recalled:

"When they brought us to the detoxifier, they opened the door and began leading us out. Suddenly, they grabbed Joseph Ahs, pulled him aside and took him away in a car. Why him? No one understood. I said then to Tolik, 'Look, he remained; he could have left and nothing would have happened.' "

Those who for one reason or another had not gone to the Central Committee waiting room began searching for the arrested. They discovered that Ahs and Chernobylsky had been separated and placed in "Sailor's Quiet," the sinister psychiatric hospital which the K.G.B. used as a prison for dissidents. They were charged with "malicious hooliganism" and the investigation had already begun.

The refuseniks quickly organized a committee, "the Group to Assist Open Public Inquiry into the Causes and Circumstances of the Arrest of Ahs and Chernobylsky." Tolik sat in jail fifteen days, came out very sick and immediately got to work: witnesses' depositions were collected, honest, courageous lawyers were hired. The committee turned to the procurator general, to the Central Committee, to all Jewish organizations abroad, to various public and academic committees. Ida Nudel, Slepak, Lerner, Tolik and others appealed to all who supported them in the West to direct all their efforts at helping Ahs and Chernobylsky. The wives of the arrested men wrote a letter to President Carter's wife, Rosalyn. Slepak received a letter of support from Jimmy Carter, and in a return one requested help for the arrested men. Tens of thousands of people from abroad sent telegrams of protest to Moscow, phoned Soviet embassies. The question was brought up at all levels. Many thought that President Carter had exerted special efforts.

Twenty days after their arrest, Ahs and Chernobylsky were released and their case closed. It was a victory. A disaster had been averted.

But the K.G.B.'s retreat was only temporary: they were planning their revenge.

A sinister baiting campaign began in the press, threats spewed forth. Many anti-Semitic articles appeared which either hinted or stated openly that all these Jewish refuseniks were enemies who were harming the Soviet Union. The articles referred to Tolik as a "gangster, prepared to take the law into his own hands." This propaganda culminated on January 22, 1977, with the television screening of the film *Buyers of Souls*, in which Tolik, Slepak and Begun [7] figured prominently. They were all called "agents of world Zionism, who are destroying the country from within." Intensive surveillance began in the winter months. Up until March, Tolik's "tails" missed only three or four days.

Ida Petrovna received a notice from the local militia reporting that a criminal case accusing Shcharansky of parasitism had been started. When Tolik had been dismissed from his job in 1974, he had tried to find other work, but

[7] Refusenik since 1971, Hebrew teacher. Dismissed from his engineering job because of his desire to emigrate, he was later arrested for parasitism and exiled for two years. When he went to visit his wife in Moscow after serving out his term, he was rearrested because his internal passport did not entitle him to spend the night in Moscow. He is now serving a second sentence of three years of exile.

like many other refuseniks he was not accepted anywhere. He then started giving private lessons in physics, mathematics and English since his diploma gave him the right to do so. When Tolik's friends heard about the police notice, they tried to convince him to write an open letter so that a campaign in his defense could be organized. He refused, saying that there were many more serious cases and he didn't want to "push himself forward."

His students' parents wrote a statement affirming that Tolik was giving lessons to their children. They traveled together to Istra and appeared before the local police. They were received with remarkable good will, their depositions were taken and a few days later a letter arrived stating that the case against Shcharansky was closed. No one understood what exactly had happened. Now it seems to me that they had already decided to take action against him, but had not yet chosen the method.

During the winter Tolik was living in the apartment of Lida Voronina, a refusenik with whom we had become friendly before I left. Since Lida lived with her friends and looked after their children, her apartment remained empty. For the eternally homeless Tolik, who lacked a permanent place to stay after Lunts's departure, this room in the center of Moscow was a real find.

In January, they searched the apartment and confiscated all my letters and pictures. Several hundred had piled up in the past two and a half years. Tolik carried them in his portfolio, with which he never parted. Dina Beilin told me later that he went around like a crushed man, constantly repeating:

"Why, why do they need these letters? They are the only thing I have. They are my life. And they took them all." Dina scolded him, saying that if these letters were so precious, then he should have kept them with his mother in Istra, and not carried them everywhere in his portfolio. He answered:

"But how could I read them then?"

At the end of January, Lida Voronina received permission and left. Again left without a place to live, Tolik temporarily moved in with the Slepaks. Tolik felt uncomfortable in their communal apartment, filled with their children, a huge dog, and other refuseniks and foreign guests who eternally crowded in for help or advice. Even without him his hosts were living in very cramped quarters. Sanya Lipavsky then proposed that he live in an apartment which he had just rented.

Dr. Sanya Lipavsky appeared in the circle of refuseniks in 1974 and quickly became his own man. Everyone considered him very likable, companionable and intelligent. Everyone particularly valued his constant willingness to help in large and small matters. He cared for the Lerners and for elderly people with heart conditions, gave them medicine, measured their blood pressure and finally became a house doctor and friend of the family. He helped people who were leaving to pack their things, to run to various offices, offered to let everyone use his car. No one ever had to ask him about something twice; he himself sought ways to help.

Little was known about his private life, except that he had received a refusal in the beginning of 1974 and had left his wife, with whom he couldn't get along. Someone said that in the sixties his father had been arrested for carrying on illegal transactions and had served a ten-year term. But this didn't interest anyone; the common practice among the refuseniks was not to delve into someone else's biography. Everyone agreed that he was a good man and that was enough. Lipavsky always spoke admiringly of Tolik, was amazed at his work capacity and tried to be helpful to him.

When I later asked Dina Beilin about Lipavsky, she suddenly remembered an episode which now, in retrospect, acquired new meaning:

"Once," she told me, "we were driving someplace with Lipavsky. It was a beautiful fall day. Everyone was silent. Suddenly he said to Tolik:

" 'Look at the beauty around us. It's a marvelous life. I'm thinking, I have just about everything: a home, car, just a little more money and I wouldn't need to go anywhere. What do you think, Tolik?'

"Tolik was immersed in his own thoughts and simply didn't hear anything. It all went by me too, and only now, after what happened, his monologues come to mind. That gesture, intonation. . . ."

When Sanya Lipavsky suggested that Tolik live in his apartment, Tolik was ready to move in immediately. Sanya replied that not everything was ready; the apartment needed some repairs. Tolik went to Joseph and Dina Beilin temporarily, then returned to the Slepaks'. The following Saturday in February, Lipavsky gave Tolik the key, explaining that he was busy with something, had to travel somewhere on business. Dina met him then at the synagogue. He stood around for a while with everyone, then said, "My feet are soaked, I'm going."

Lipavsky disappeared after that. Tolik didn't succeed in living with him in his comfortable, "fixed-up" apartment. On March 4, sudden searches were carried out in the apartments of seven Jewish families—the Lerners, the Beilins, the Slepaks, Ida Nudel, Chernobylsky, Kremen, and Lipavsky's apartment where Tolik planned to live. As soon as they had finished the search in her house, Dina Beilin immediately went to the Lerners'. She already knew that the same thing was taking place there and feared for the health of these two cardiac cases, especially since their "home doctor," Sanya Lipavsky, had disappeared; no one knew where to find him. Everyone stood around and silently watched the K.G.B. agents storm the Lerners' apartment. The man in charge of the search looked at them, smirked and coldbloodedly said:

"Don't get excited, this is all child's play. What joy awaits you tomorrow, what joy! Tomorrow will be the happiest day in your life!"

After the search, Dina went out to buy the evening newspaper, *Izvestiya*; she opened it and froze: on the third page she read the headline: "To the Presidium of the Supreme Soviet, copy to the U.S. Congress and to the U.N. Open Letter of Citizen of the U.S.S.R. Lipavsky." In his letter of "confession," Lipavsky wrote that he publicly renounced his formal request to emigrate to Israel because he considered his only homeland to be the Soviet Union. He accused all his former refusenik friends of serving and being in the hire of the American counterintelligence service. He named as the leaders of this espionage net David Azbel, Alexander Lerner, Vitaly Rubin. The article enumerated Shcharansky, Lunts and M. Azbel as active participants. The Slepaks were also mentioned. Lipavsky wrote that he had been forcibly enlisted by the C.I.A., but now repented and asked for forgiveness.

The entire sixth page of the newspaper was a supplement to Lipavsky's letter entitled "The C.I.A., Spies and Human Rights." Some anonymous writers gave details of Lipavsky's biography. Everything was told in a cloudy, mysterious, incomprehensible way as in a cheap detective novel—how he had concealed some information in some hiding places, fragments of some "coded letters" were cited as an example. This supplement also contained a real attack against the American journalists accredited in Moscow and against workers in the American embassy. All of them—Melvin Lewitzky, Joseph Pressel, Peter Osnos, Joseph Krimski and others—were called spies.

Everyone read the paper silently; no one could utter a word. . . . Clearly, the authorities had worked out a plan of reprisal against the Jewish movement and these articles were only the first step. It had never entered anyone's head that Lipavsky was an agent provocateur.

A real siege started the next morning. Cars stood by the homes of all the refuseniks. The Slepaks' home, where Tolik was then living, was cordoned off. The K.G.B. agents stood in every stairwell, at the entrance and by the apartment door. Almost all of the refuseniks' telephones were disconnected.

Trying not to give in to the mood of terror, Tolik joked:

"They've raised my title—from hooligan and parasite I've risen to spy."

Everyone understood that not only those directly mentioned in the article—Lerner, Slepak, Shcharansky and M. Azbel (Lunts, Rubin and D. Azbel had already left Russia some time ago)—but also all refuseniks were in danger. If those mentioned were arrested and condemned, all who knew them or simply met them at some time would automatically be considered guilty. From there it would be one step to labeling all those who wanted to go to Israel as spies.

Sensing an impending catastrophe, the friends gathered in the Slepaks' home, recalling the Doctors' Plot in Stalin's time and the Dreyfus affair in France, and spoke of a similar scenario.

Many felt it was symbolic that the newspaper article appeared on Purim:

"Haman again found a suitable time to take reprisals against us. Please God that it ends this time as it did in Persia three thousand years ago."

They recalled that another Haman—Stalin—who had concocted the "Doctors' Plot," which was to have been the "final solution to the Jewish question in Russia," did not fully succeed in carrying out his intention because on Purim in 1953 he died.

The days went by. Rumors spread that they would take Lerner first. In the meantime, they didn't take anyone, but the tails became more and more unceremonious and brazen. Eight or nine uniformed men encircled Tolik when he left the house. His friends never left him alone, accompanied him everywhere, but the K.G.B. men surrounded him, pushed the others away and didn't let him talk to anyone. During this time he went out to try and telephone me, but the call never went through.

His friend Feliks Kandel later told me:

"I saw him for the last time on Saturday at the synagogue.

His tails had become completely subhuman; they stood in a tight ring around him. I said to them, 'Nu, get away, why are you interfering?' but they didn't answer, they only stood and looked at him, like jackals. Then we began to leave the synagogue. And I said, 'Tolya, well, good luck.' And he left somehow doomed, as if he had made a great personal effort to go. He didn't want to leave the synagogue, the crowd. He seemed to feel that he was going away into something, in those years. And all that horde, a semicircle of about eight men behind him."

Ten days passed, and they hadn't arrested anyone. It seemed as if it had passed: "they" had had second thoughts.

On the morning of March 15, someone came to Slepak and reported that they had let out Dr. Stern.[8] Tolik was so happy that he ran out of the apartment without his coat to phone everyone with the news. Slepak ran after him, but the K.G.B. men guarding the door threw him out of the elevator, pushed Tolik in and went in after him. Slepak ran down the stairs three at a time trying to overtake the elevator.

A few minutes later he returned, pale with trembling lips: "They took him away." He couldn't say anything else.

The news quickly flew around Moscow. People immediately began coming in. Toward evening they phoned the "on-duty K.G.B." Ordinarily, they never speak with anyone there, but this time they answered:

"Shcharansky? He's with us!"

The following morning Sakharov called all the foreign correspondents to his home. Friends, acquaintances arrived. There was no place to stand in the apartment. After Sakharov read out the declaration and told correspondents all the circumstances of Tolya's arrest, no one left. Silence filled the

---

[8] An elderly doctor accused of bribetaking, who had already served over three years of his prison sentence. Tolik had been active in helping his wife and in gathering material to prove Stern's innocence.

room; everyone was overwhelmed. It was as if everyone in that room experienced personal grief.

Natulya, my beloved, my joy.

A week has passed and I am gradually getting used to my new "spy career," to the continual presence of "bodyguards" by the doors, to living without possessions and papers (all my documents were confiscated).

The first night after the *Izvestiya* article, when I had to adjust to this new life and to new earthly categories, I realized very clearly, as never before, how horrible and senseless my whole life has been without you.

How everything has changed over these past days. Thousands of things and words which used to fill my life have simply disappeared, ceased to exist. Only the most important and dearest thing to me remains—you and our love. A lucidity sets in, when you live not by the minute nor the day, but your whole life at once.

Thinking about it all, I regretted only one thing—so much so that I was ready to cry: I regretted that we didn't have any children.

Now I have calmed down a little, my thoughts are composed, and I am sure that we shall soon have them. Do you think so, too?

I think I would be completely calm were I not fearful for you. How can I reassure you, how can I comfort you? Natulya, no matter what happens to me now, in the end everything will be all right, please try to understand and believe this. Take care of your health and nerves.

I am living now at the Slepaks' apartment; my tails live by the door. They have camped out in the courtyard and in the entryway. I went into the "nursery" [9] to write this letter, and while I was writing, around eight people showed up in

---

[9] The room previously used by the Slepaks' now grown-up children.

the large room, each of whom needs me for something important.

Mama is holding up pretty well, but I fear that when the tension lets up a horrible reaction will set in. Papa is taking it very hard. He doesn't sleep, his heart aches, his blood pressure jumped way up and I fear that he won't live through all of this.

I received your letter after a long break—it came to Istra and Mama brought it to me. What you say to me there now sounds especially significant and important. I hope to speak to you this evening; then everything will become easier right away. After we talk on the phone I promise to sit down and write you a long letter and I'll send it so that it gets to you.[10]

I kiss you, my joy, my happiness.

A postscript by Ida Petrovna on the back of the above letter:

Natashenka, my dear! I don't have my glasses with me so I'm writing blindly. You understand my condition, just as I understand yours. Yet I don't cease hoping for the best. We are always with you in our thoughts and yearn for a reunion.

My wonderful girl! How I want to see and hear you! Please try to write! Boris Moiseyevich [11] and everyone send regards and join in all my wishes. Tolik, as always, is a real hero! He speaks about you a lot and dreams about the long-awaited time.

Try to be calmer and have faith that truth shall triumph. I embrace you, kiss you, love you and miss you very much.

Yours,
Ida Petrovna

[10] Anatoly refers to his intention to send the letter with a private individual since letters sent through the mail did not arrive.

[11] Anatoly's father.

The Dash

I didn't find out about all this until later. While the K.G.B. agents were conducting their searches in Moscow and trembling Jewish hands opened up the evening edition of *Izvestiya*, we in Jerusalem were busily preparing for the Purim holiday. The house smelled of poppy seeds, roasted almonds and pies. Ilana and I baked, cooked and prepared paper plates filled with treats for friends and neighbors. Hannale, dressed as Pippi Longstocking, with braids sticking out in all directions and huge happy eyes, ran around the neighborhood distributing our *sholach monos* gift plates. The door would ring and some small pirate with a glued-on mustache or an adult in a sombrero would run in for a minute to greet us and give us the *sholach monos* from his family. On the table the heap of plates prepared by us diminished as the pile of gifts sent to us grew. We were almost drunk from excitement on that Purim, a holiday which combines carefree rejoicing and faith in miracles, reliance on God, and terrible tragedy, which recurs all too often—the threat of our people's annihilation.

The morning paper lay on the sofa like a time bomb ready at any minute to tear apart our holiday. But no one looked at it. Only on the following evening did Benjamin open it and turn pale: "Read."

The report of Lipavsky's letter was meager but sufficiently exact to make everything clear at once. I felt a strange chill: slander, the "blood libel." Again the Dreyfus case, the Doctors' Plot. Haman. All these terrible, familiar phrases swam into my head.

But Tolik, my Tolik in the midst of this! Against him and his friends! My God! What can be done? What will happen?

I wanted to run out into the street and to scream!

"They started this before! This has already happened before!"

But I couldn't move. The three of us sat for a long time, immersed in the gloom of twilight without speaking. A knock on the door brought us back to life: our friends Tzvi and Hannah had arrived.

Their visits in the evening after the Sabbath had long since become a tradition. They came with a huge bag full of books. On the table there soon appeared a volume of the Talmud, works of some medieval Jewish philosophers and invariably the works of Rabbi Abraham Isaac Kook, whom they considered their spiritual teacher.

These lessons usually ended well after midnight, but even after their departure we would sit for a long time discussing what we had heard, trying to understand and to familiarize ourselves with the world which had been opened up to us that evening. Each lesson really seemed that way to us.

But this time our friends immediately saw that something had happened. We didn't need to explain our story; it was all familiar and clear.

"Yes, it has happened before. And more than once."

"Something has to be done," said Tzvi quietly, addressing himself more than us.

"What?"

"I don't know yet. Meanwhile, let us look at something in our books. We shall find strength and study a little. Later we shall decide."

The Shcharansky family. From left: Leonid, Mrs. Milgrom, Anatoly, Boris Shcharansky

Anatoly at age 9

Anatoly in high school (1963)

Anatoly in Moscow (1975)

Avital in Sweden (1977)

Professor Alexander Lerner and Mrs. Ida Milgrom in Moscow, during Anatoly's trial

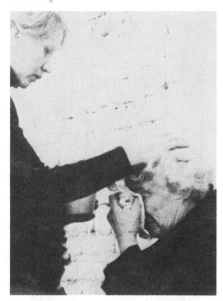

Mrs. Milgrom and Leonid Shcharansky's wife Raya, after hearing Anatoly's sentence

From left to right: Professor V. Rubin, V. Slepack, D. Azrel, Col. Lev Ovsischer, I. Beilin, Anatoly Shcharansky, D. Beilin, I. Nudel, Professor A. Lerner

Anatoly Shcharansky (1975)

The Sterns

Vladimir Slepack, Moscow, 1977

Synagogue in Moscow where Soviet Jews often gather for informal meetings

KGB interrogation prison, Lefortovo, Moscow. Anatoly was interrogated here for 16 months prior to the trial, from March 15,
1977 to July 8, 1978

Two visiting American lawyers discuss Anatoly's situation with Anatoly's family. From left: Professor Piter Liacouras, Mrs. Ida Milgrom, Mrs. Dina Beilin, Professor Burton Caine, Leonid Shcharansky (Anatoly's brother). Moscow, December, 1977

Avital meeting with Willie Brandt, June 1977, Rome

Demonstration in Antwerp, summer of 1977

Demonstration in New York, summer 1977

Avital meets with Elie Wiesel, August 1977

Avital with George Meany, summer 1977

Ad hoc committee for Shcharansky, Washington, D.C., October 20, 1977. From left: Al Friendly, Professor Jack Minker, Isaak Elkind, Avital Shcharansky

Avital at a TV interview in Boston, March 1978

Press conference with "Scientists for Shcharansky" in San Francisco, immediately after the trial, July, 1978

Telephone conversation with Mrs. Milgrom, Boston, 1978

Avital at M.I.T., 1978

Avital with Joan Baez at Berkeley rally, July 1978

Telephone conversation with Mrs. Milgrom, 1978

Press conference with Congressman Robert Drinan, March 15, 1979. From left: Michael Stieglitz (Avital's brother), Avital, Drinan.

Arkhipov Street on Saturday afternoon. A crowd is gathered as usual outside the synagogue.

It was difficult for me to follow the lesson that evening. Tzvi and Hannah left after midnight. Instead of going to sleep, we began to think about whom to call and where to send telegrams.

Around three o'clock in the morning we heard cautious steps on the stairs, hesitation in front of our door, a quiet knock. Tzvi had returned. He brought with him a bearded, solid short man with burning eyes.

"Meet Yankele, he is one of those who know how 'to do things.'"

Yankele questioned me about everything for a long time, agitatedly pacing from corner to corner. Light was already dawning when he said:

"Yes, we must do something." We must act immediately; it is very easy to lose time. It's already morning. You sleep a little, and in the evening come with your brother to Kiryat Moshe, we'll find some apartment, sit down and discuss *tachlis*.[1] This apartment doesn't even have a telephone; it's impossible without a telephone.

That was March 5.

The following day we met in a small, modest apartment in Kiryat Moshe, the area of Jerusalem in which the yeshiva of Rabbi Kook is located. The only wealth and adornment in the apartment were books and children. Benny, the young, black-bearded owner of the apartment, sent his six children to their beds and his wife, Sarah, prepared tea and coffee for the guests. Yankele was already waiting for us. Other friends of Tzvi arrived; some were rabbis or yeshiva students, vaguely familiar or complete strangers to me.

The talk went in circles, continually returning to the point that this was a very serious matter and the danger was great. Everyone agreed that not only those mentioned in the article nor only those subjected to searches were in

---

[1] "Goals" in Yiddish.

danger but all the refuseniks, and, if one dug deeper, Russian Jewry as a whole.

Around eleven o'clock that night we decided to call Lunts and Rubin, the chief "spies" mentioned in the article, to hear their opinion. Benny went somewhere, borrowed a car and brought them to us. We all sat together until three in the morning considering what we could do. One thing was clear. We had to make noise. We had to unmask the K.G.B.'s plans to the whole world as soon as possible.

Work began in the morning. First we called all our friends abroad. We tried to establish contact with Moscow, to reach Tolik by telephone. We sought new contacts in Europe and America. People searched their memories for relatives and friends: someone is a journalist in London, someone is the head of the Jewish community in Geneva. Names were brought up, faces flitted past, the telephone worked incessantly. Around dinnertime they brought in a second telephone line from a neighbor's house. I couldn't understand anything.

Yankele directed all this activity; he stood like an army commander in the middle of the room, gave orders, rang up some acquaintances.

We gathered again in the evening, to discuss everything. It was decided to arrange a press conference.

"There are dozens of accredited correspondents from all parts of the globe in Israel. We have to try and see that they all come," ordered Yankele.

From seven in the morning, two people sat by the telephone, informing, cajoling and convincing representatives from the press, radio and television to come. Others translated items into Hebrew and English and prepared material for publication on everything mentioned in *Izvestiya*. Someone went to arrange for a press room at Beit Agron. Someone else distributed press releases to all the newspapers. A box stood on the table and everyone emptied their pockets.

People continually kept arriving, asking for news and

offering to help. Seeing the box on the table, they would put some money in. A small fund thus accumulated.

All day we used taxis from the nearby taxi stand until one of the drivers simply drove his car up to the house.

"I am at your service. My working day is over. I can help."

The correspondent from *Maariv* [2] arrived at midnight. A day later the first serious article about the events in Moscow appeared in that paper.

The whole night through we prepared for the press conference. Toward morning we woke up the owner of the printing press. He needed less than five hours to print two hundred copies of all the biographies in two languages, photographs and other material.

Everything was prepared in one day. I began to understand what it means to "do something."

Our first press conference took place at ten o'clock in the morning. The participants included Lunts, Rubin, Berta Rozhovskaya (the mother of Maria Slepak), Sonya Lerner (the daughter of A. Lerner) and me. The room was overflowing with people. All the press people whom we had invited appeared. For two hours we explained, answered questions.

By noon the news report already mentioned the press conference. After it, we all went together to the Chief Rabbi of Israel, Rabbi Goren. He understood everything:

"Jews are in danger."

He immediately composed a telegram for Moscow, President Carter, the Pope and Jewish communities around the world. The radio transmitted his appeal to pray on the next Sabbath for Soviet Jews.

Evenings were followed by days, everything merged in this crazy work, a feeling of time disappeared. I didn't have time to sleep, eat or think. Only one desire constantly tormented me: I had to speak to Tolik. To hear his voice, to tell him

2 An Israeli newspaper.

that I am with him, that I will be with him forever, no matter what happens. I called endlessly to his parents in Istra, tried to phone all of Tolik's Moscow friends that I knew—all in vain. The telephones in Moscow were disconnected.

Moscow Jews succeeded in breaking through to us on March 9, via London, where an appeal with 250 signatures was received. Michael Sherbourne, a London friend of Soviet refuseniks, immediately phoned us. In a voice bursting with emotion he read the appeal from Moscow.

"We appeal to you at one of the most dramatic and perhaps decisive moments in the history of Russian Jewry. Our grandfathers' lifetime was marred by the somber period of the Beilis case.

"The case of the so-called doctors-murderers filled our fathers' lives like a suffocating nightmare. Now in our lifetime they are preparing a new case, 'the case of the spies,' bringing to our mind the notorious case of the 'spy and traitor' Dreyfus. Recently we have seen a swift escalation of pressure on the Jews: the beating in the forest, mass arrests for fifteen days, efforts to intimidate in various cities, the arrest of Begun in Moscow, the trial of Zavurov [3] in Uzbekistan, the case of Salansky [4] in Vilna. And finally, the monstrous libel on the pages of *Izvestiya*.

"Only a small part of the iceberg is visible. All the rest is hidden, concealed until the time is ripe. What is being prepared there in secret? We don't know yet. But we shall soon

[3] Having completed all the necessary forms and received permission to emigrate, he was on his way from his native Dushanbe to Moscow. At the Dushanbe airport, police suddenly stopped him and asked for his passport, which they did not return. Before he could board the plane, he was arrested for not having a passport. When he objected to this in the police station, they added a further count of resisting arrest. He was sentenced to three years at a labor camp.

[4] A participant in a seminar on Jewish culture in Vilna. He was arrested for anti-Soviet propaganda on the basis of his participation in this seminar. After Western academics started a campaign on his behalf, the case was closed.

feel it. This is no longer a reprisal against individual refuseniks. All of Russian Jewry is being discredited and defamed in the best traditions of tsarist and Stalinist times. The catchwords have already been affixed: 'Jew-spy,' 'traitor,' 'renegade.' From there it is not far to a noisy trial, to an uncontrolled outbreak of the 'popular masses.' We already hear the reverberations on the streets, in the subway, in the stores.

"Yesterday only the refuseniks were hostages. Today all the Jews of the U.S.S.R. became hostages.

"Friends! Brothers!

"In this difficult hour of our life we want everyone to know: no betrayals, no threats and no libel will intimidate us. They will not force us to turn back in our struggle for human dignity. We are proud of our past and present. We shall do our utmost not to discredit the honor and dignity of our people in the future. *Am Yisroel chai!* (The nation of Israel lives!)"

We found out from the newspapers that a meeting of the Executive Committee of the Brussels Conference for the Defense of Soviet Jewry would open in Geneva in two days. I must be there! This appeal must sound forth there!

The Ministry of Foreign Affairs in Tel-Aviv agreed to send Michael and me there only if we succeeded in obtaining passports and tickets in such a short time.

At the *mateh* (headquarters), as Benny and Sarah's apartment was now being called, they prepared the documents for our trip; they translated the appeal, and contacted people all over the world. We went with Yankele to the Interior Ministry, where they were already closing. It didn't take long to explain why he had come: we wanted a passport. It normally takes a month to get one; this time it took fifteen minutes.

That night the whole group went to visit Rabbi Tzvi Yehuda Kook, the eighty-year-old son of Rabbi Abraham

Isaac Kook, whose books we studied with Tzvi and Hannah on Saturday evenings. All the people who were so devoted to helping us in those days were students of the rabbi. Trying to be as quiet as we could, we arrived at his small apartment, which was lined from floor to ceiling with books. The rabbi was ill and lay in bed in the far corner of the room propped up on high pillows. Chairs stood in a semicircle near his bed.

We told him everything and read him the appeal. He became agitated, and ordered us to call all his students whom he thought could help and ask them to come forth. Late that night, the people who had answered his call from various cities gathered around his bed. It was decided temporarily to close the yeshiva in which some were teaching and others studying in order to concentrate all efforts on preventing the K.G.B.'s expected revenge.

"If your brother is in danger and you ask, 'How can I help?' you are like one who spills blood. Don't ask! Go and do!"

Thus the rabbi spoke. He blessed Michael and me and wished us success in our journey; his benediction seemed to give us new strength.

In the morning in Tel-Aviv we learned that our tickets were ready and the plane would leave in two hours. We didn't have time to go home. Chomi answered when we phoned the *mateh*. Small, dark-haired, large-eyed Chomi sat by the telephone day and night all last week. Where had she come from? Why did all this upset her so much that she wouldn't agree to go home to sleep even for a few hours? Looking at her pale, sunken face, I wondered, Who is she, this Sabra? And why did I have the feeling that I had known her for so long? All these questions hung in the air—there was no time for an explanation.

"Chomi, we're flying in two hours. It's cold in Europe and we don't even have a change of underwear. What should we do?"

"Don't get upset. Let's go to the airport. We'll think of something."

She went to Ilana and the two of them packed a suitcase in fifteen minutes and rode to the airport. Israeli television was already waiting for us there. We left on March 13 for Geneva, after a hasty interview, having arrived late for the flight and with only forty dollars in our pockets.

I ran up the stairs; the friends who had accompanied us remained below. I glanced around: Yankele stood resolutely, stroking his beard, Benny was smiling, Chomi shouted "Shalom!" and Ilana, turning pale, looked at us silently.

Memories flashed through my head:

Moscow, Sheremetevo Airport, Tolik . . .

With the appeal in our hands, we literally ran into the conference room on the morning of March 14. After the reading, complete silence reigned.

We spent the whole day in lengthy conversations with the various participants at the conference. We were invited to come to England as quickly as possible by the London National Council for Soviet Jewry and by the group the 35's Women's Campaign for Soviet Jewry. The National Conference on Soviet Jewry invited us to New York.

Ilana called from Jerusalem to say that she had succeeded in talking to Tolik. His voice was very tense. He was terribly upset that he didn't get to speak to me. At the end of the conversation he said, "The K.G.B. is spreading rumors that they'll take Lerner first . . . And then me."

"Whatever happens, you should know that we here are fighting for you," answered Ilana. "And we shall continue all the time, day and night, until we hear from you that the danger has passed."

We spent another day in Geneva, gave our first interview to the French newspaper *Le Monde*, met with young people, and agreed on possible immediate actions with prominent Jewish figures from various countries. We seemed to have succeeded in getting something moving.

Toward evening, we heard that the Reuters correspondent in Geneva was looking for us everywhere. He asked us to come to the press center at the U.N. building right away. We got there by taxi in four minutes. We were met by a very pale man with the sorrowful face of one who had just suffered a family tragedy. He led us silently to the teletype, out of which a ribbon noisily spilled out. I tried to read it:

"Today, March 15 in the morning, Dr. Stern was released—"

Michael, leaning over my shoulder, pushed me away. "Let me look. You won't understand anything in English anyway."

He quickly pulled out the ribbon and turned to the correspondent, who was paralyzed with dismay. Then he looked at me and as if in passing, threw out:

"Tolik is arrested—"

"Is there anything else there?"

"No. Only that Stern was freed and Tolik arrested. That's all."

Tolik is the first. They have locked him in a cell. They want to destroy him and he can't even defend himself. Now I am left alone. No, on the contrary. I feel his presence very strongly, more strongly than ever before. Now he is inside me, and I am his voice, his mind, his hands, his soul . . . Everything is now on me. Everything depends on me. They won't let him defend himself. I must fight for two.

In Jerusalem they already knew everything. The *mateh* began to work on London and America. They sought out new contacts in order to extend the wave of protests as much as possible. The *mateh* itself grew; there were branches in the four major Israeli cities. Demonstrations were planned, placards and appeals printed; more and more people came to offer help.

They told us that they had phoned Menachem Begin at night—he was then in Brussels. Begin thanked them for not hesitating to waken him, because he considered it a very serious matter. He wrote a letter to Carter and gave the names of some people in Paris who might be able to help.

Through him they quickly arranged for me to meet with a representative of the French Parliament, Alain Poher. The group decided to send us a helper, Eli, one of those energetic young people who had spent days and nights in the *mateh*. I was to fly to Paris and meet Eli there and Michael would fly to London, where a demonstration had already been planned in front of the Soviet embassy and a large press conference been organized. We would all meet in London and then, leaving Eli in Europe, we would go to America.

Now, as I look back on those days, I seem to see an endless movie reel: meetings, unfamiliar faces, halls where I speak. Now I am traveling in a huge bus to the square in front of Les Invalides. From my former "museum" life I recognize the Parisian streets with sonorous names as they flash by. Then it is London and damp snow. I sit by the entrance to the Soviet embassy wrapped in some warm blankets. I have been fasting for three days. I am at the end of my strength; I feel I am about to lose consciousness. Meanwhile the passersby hurry along: someone smiles at me, someone signs the petition which is next to me on a small table. This table is heaped with flowers, the Londoners' way of expressing their sympathy with me. San Francisco. A huge crowd is crying out: "Free Anatoly Shcharansky." I see everything as if in a dream; picture follows picture, and behind each sequence a dry voice reports:

March 16. Three hundred French intellectuals—academics and writers—published a petition in defense of Anatoly Shcharansky.

More than one hundred congressmen and senators sent letters and telegrams to Carter and Brezhnev.

March 17. Student protest demonstrations took place in New York, Ottawa and London.

Andrey Sakharov sent a letter to President Carter requesting that he come to Shcharansky's defense.

In an extraordinary session the Israeli Knesset appealed to the parliaments of all countries to come to Shcharansky's defense and to prevent reprisals against Soviet Jews.

March 21. Over ten thousand people turned out for demonstrations in Israel. Participants included the mayors of several cities, Golda Meir, Chief Rabbi Goren, Yigal Allon, members of the Knesset.

Demonstrations in Los Angeles, Baltimore, San Francisco, Washington, New York, Paris, London, Montreal . . .

After America I travel around Europe for two months at an incredible pace: France, Germany, England, Holland, Belgium, Italy.

In Paris they organize a committee for the defense of Shcharansky. A prominent French mathematician, Professor Laurent Schwartz, joins our struggle as the initiator of many actions. In Holland I receive assurances of support from the Minister of Foreign Affairs. In England the Archbishop of Canterbury and many other prominent churchmen come out in defense of Tolik. In mid-May I meet the members of European parliaments in Strasbourg. Then a meeting with Willy Brandt. A letter from German Chancellor Helmut Schmidt that he is "carefully following the development of events and promises help."

The Shcharansky case is discussed in the English Parliament.

This list could go on forever. During all this time I dash from country to country—some places invite me; others I go to at my own cost and risk. My itinerary might appear chaotic, but, in fact, there was clear logic to it. I keep a constant telephone contact with our *mateh*. They have long since moved home to San Simon. Ilana succeeded in getting a telephone in a very short time and now all the planning and coordination of my trips originates from there.

Our friends from Kiryat Moshe returned to their yeshiva

teaching and studies. They accomplished something very important: they gave us a push, taught us what it means "to do something." The yeshiva couldn't remain empty. Now we ourselves must toil away, not thinking about time, competing with the Soviets in endurance. Still, people continuously come to Ilana and Benjamin's house to offer help. Chomi, in fact, moved in, completely putting aside her own personal life. She typed, translated, was on call. Little Hannale learned to care for herself. The house was constantly overflowing with people. When Michael returned from America, he quickly joined in the work.

In Jerusalem they were living under the same tension as I. I felt that I had a home front, a coordinating center. I was not alone.

Nobody could find out anything about Tolik during all this time. Occasionally I succeeded in getting through to Istra. Tolik's aged father couldn't withstand the stress and lay ill with a serious heart condition. Ida Petrovna held up by some sort of miracle. She lived, no doubt, just as I did, on adrenalin, completely forgetting about herself, thinking only of Tolik. She wrote letters to the K.G.B., to the Supreme Soviet, to Brezhnev demanding that they explain to her why her son had been arrested. The authorities maintained complete silence. The only fact we had was that Tolik was being kept in a solitary cell in the Lefortovo Prison, the most terrible of all the K.G.B. prisons.

In mid-May we heard rumors that interrogations had begun in Moscow on the Shcharansky case. Those questioned reported that the interrogators had tried intimidation and threats to obtain testimony about espionage, state treason and a secret Jewish organization in Moscow. During the interrogation of Benjamin Fain, a man entered the office, said that he had the authority to decide whether Fain received permission to leave for Israel, and if Fain would give the necessary testimony he would receive a visa;

if not, he would wind up behind bars. With Brailovsky they threatened to call a car and send him to prison. Often people were subjected to preventive arrest. Sometimes they were held there for twelve hours without a break. The interrogators, cynical to the utmost, would often declare: "This case is being conducted not in the interest of justice but for state interests," or, "This is a political measure of national proportions."

And, in fact, interrogations in the Shcharansky case began in various cities all around the Soviet Union. They called in people who had never seen Tolik. They intimidated them, trying to force them to slander themselves and their friends. Newspaper articles in Kiev and Minsk made accusations against local refuseniks similar to those contained in Lipavsky's letter in *Izvestiya*. Interrogators from Odessa, Kiev, Dushanbe and other cities were present at the Moscow interrogations. But the Jews stood firmly: no one agreed to slander Tolik. Neither threats nor promises had any effect, no one was broken. One of the refuseniks who were questioned—Leonid Volvovsky—wrote in the protocol of the interrogation:

"I hope that Shcharansky, when he signs the document at the end of the investigation, can read my testimony. Since he has been accused of betraying his homeland, I would like him to know that his homeland remembers him and prays for him. It prays that the Almighty will strengthen his resolve, mind and conscience. . . ."

In July, K.G.B. agents arrested the American correspondent from the *Los Angeles Times*, Robert Toth, one of the foreign journalists whose name had been mentioned in *Izvestiya*. His three-year service in Moscow was then just ending. Tickets had been ordered for his flight, the family was packing their bags. They grabbed him on the street, brought him to the K.G.B. and accused him of receiving secret information. Forbidding him to leave the U.S.S.R., they forced him to appear for questioning at Lefortovo. They questioned him for thirteen hours on his connections with Shcharansky. The interrogation was conducted through a translator. At the end, they gave him a text typed up in Russian to sign. Toth objected that he couldn't put his signature on a document whose contents he didn't understand, since he didn't know Russian. They politely explained to him that "in accordance with Soviet law he did not have the right to refuse to sign the protocol." He trustingly signed and they immediately removed the arrest warrant. When he returned to America and consulted with his lawyer, he found out that they had simply deceived him. He then sent a sworn statement to the prosecutor general of the Soviet Union in which he declared that he had been interrogated under pressure and through a ruse been forced to sign the protocol.

When news appeared about the interrogations, everyone, even those who had doubted up to then, realized that the K.G.B. was contriving a big case whose goal was to take measures against the Jewish emigration movement and to throw a shadow on all Russian Jewry. No one needed proof any longer.

At the time the interrogations were being conducted in the U.S.S.R., I was traveling through Europe. The beginning of June found me in Italy. The warm blue sky and bright sun reminded me that I was in the Mediterranean, close to Israel. But I didn't allow myself to weaken. I had a heavy schedule of meetings and appearances. Residing in a small hotel, I felt very exhausted and alone. I didn't understand Italian and couldn't even give instructions to the porter.

Israelis living in Rome wanted to help me, but from tiredness and some kind of internal emptiness, I didn't know how to get down to work. I called home. "Please try to send someone to help me."

I found out on the following day that Michael Fern was coming. He was born in France, knew European languages and was a very reliable person. I felt better right away.

On the way to the airport, I became upset: "Who is he? How shall I talk to him? I don't know him; I don't even know what he looks like."

The passengers went by one after the other to pick up their luggage.

"Perhaps it's that elderly man? No. He isn't looking for anyone. That one? No—his face is too 'alien.'"

Suddenly I saw a middle-aged man with resolute movements, a light beard and a sharp, stern gaze in his bright blue eyes. He came directly to me. "Shalom, Avital. I am Michael. I've come from Jerusalem to help you. What is going on here?"

I looked at him and I already felt at ease. This emissary from Israel seemed to me an angel sent by God Himself to give me strength. In the car he listened to my account of matters without interrupting me. All this was new for him. He worked with young people in the problem areas of Jerusalem. He was about to start his army reserve service when my friends came asking for his help. He immediately agreed and on the same day he managed to settle matters at work and in the army, packed his suitcase, said goodbye to his wife and children for ten days, and flew to Rome.

These ten days turned into two months. He gave me confidence and strength; now I had a mouthpiece and could work more effectively. From Rome we went to France, Belgium and Denmark. But all that was later. In Rome I spent the whole evening telling him about my trips and problems and about the interrogations in Moscow.

The telephone rang early in the morning. From Moscow came a report that Ida Petrovna had received a letter from the prosecutor of the U.S.S.R. which stated that her son, Anatoly Shcharansky, was accused of espionage and treason according to article 64 of the Criminal Code of the U.S.S.R. The punishment: fifteen years of prison or the death sentence.

The telephone started ringing and never stopped. Correspondents began arriving at the hotel. One television crew replaced the other. In the breaks between interviews I tried to call Istra; I wanted to comfort Tolik's parents, to assure them that the very worst would not occur. I didn't have time to think about Tolik and me.

An appeal to all the Jewish communities in the world was transmitted from Moscow:

"Brothers and sisters!

"The Moscow Jew. Anatoly Shcharansky is threatened with long years of imprisonment or with the death penalty!

"The K.G.B. is conducting the investigation into his case secretly and without the use of a lawyer.

"Using the mass media, the K.G.B. is spreading the information that Anatoly Shcharansky and other Jewish refuseniks are agents of the American counterintelligence. These reports are as absurd as the Stalinist lie about the 'Jewish cosmopolitans' in 1949 or the 'doctors-poisoners' in 1953. They are again trying to sacrifice the Jews to the dark instincts of the masses. They again hope to paralyze with fear hundreds of thousands of Jewish souls before whom a road had been opened toward reunification with their brothers and with their God.

"Brothers and sisters!

"The Shcharansky case is not a mistake and not a political trick as one could have hoped not long ago.

"It is a definite stage in the escalation of hatred. It is a threat of death for one, the threat of deprivation of freedom for hundreds, the threat of demoralization and the loss of the remnants of national dignity for millions of Soviet Jews.

"Brothers and sisters!

"You cannot be indifferent. For God led both you and me out of Egypt. It was your blood and mine which boiled in the ovens of Maidanek.

"Your hair and mine turned gray in Entebbe. You and I, together with the prisoners of Zion, cut down forests in the Gulag Archipelago.

"You and I today are in the cell of the Moscow K.G.B. prison along with Anatoly Shcharansky.

"Our house is again filled with misfortune.

"But no matter how great the evil, God is greater. He has given us the patience of Job. He will also give us the spirit of Rabbi Akiva."

The news that Tolik would be tried according to article 64 caused a tremendous stir throughout the world. Newspapers and magazines were filled with articles and reports on the Shcharansky case.

Hundreds of petitions were sent to Soviet representatives abroad and in Moscow. Almost every day meetings and demonstrations took place in various cities around the globe.

A group of American students offered themselves in exchange for Tolik.

Fourteen New York rabbis chained themselves to the fence of the Soviet Mission to the U.N. Rabbis and priests in San Francisco took part in a similar action there. Stormy demonstrations took place in the quiet city of Antwerp.

Petitions and protests came from Venezuela, Brazil, Mexico, New Zealand, Japan. News about the Shcharansky case was published even in Singapore and the Philippines, and in the Lebanese press and news.

In Paris an invitation was waiting to come to Washington for a few days. A big meeting was planned in which all those to whom we had turned for help planned to take part. I flew to Washington.

Thousands of people gathered in the huge hall, filled to overflowing. I faced Tolik's and my own friends from various states, official representatives of the American establishment—many familiar and unfamiliar attentive eyes. I controlled my voice with difficulty.

My God! If it were not for Tolik. Were it not for the thought of the terrible danger hanging over his life, I could never withstand this tension, this ordeal, to stand here on this podium.

I asked everyone who was listening to me to appeal to President Carter, to intercede for my husband.

In the evening this huge crowd of thousands of people went with candles through the dark city to the Washington Monument. People came up to me to encourage me, give me hope.

In a television appearance on the morning of June 13, President Carter said that he had personally carefully checked everything connected with the accusation of espionage against Shcharansky, and he declared that it was false.

On June 30, the American House and Senate unanimously, with no abstentions, accepted a special resolution sharply condemning the U.S.S.R. for the Shcharansky case.

On the initiative of Congressman Robert Drinan, an International Committee for the Release of Anatoly Shcharansky was formed at the end of June. It included several hundred members of parliaments, social and religious leaders, lawyers, academics, and writers from the U.S.A., Canada and England.

I returned to Europe and with Michael Fern continued to travel from country to country, finding understanding and support everywhere. This state of tension kept up until the end of July. I was completely exhausted. I desperately needed a "gulp of Israel"; otherwise I simply couldn't hold up any longer. Michael Fern was also tired. He thought that we had done everything that we could. Now we had to do a lot of thinking and consult with friends. We decided to return home.

Ilana hugged me: "Well, thank God, you made it home."
Hannale ran to meet me: "Did you already free Tolik?"
Tolik looked at me from posters and photographs on the

walls. The house was full of piles of papers and bundles. Typewriters stood on the floor, in the corners, the telephone rang incessantly.

Flexing his muscles, which were numb from endless sitting, my brother Michael crawled in from the balcony, where he was sifting through papers and piles of letters.

"Are you still alive? Quick: take a bath and get to bed!"

How good it is to be home. I can permit myself to lie down and not move.

Benjamin, the only breadwinner for our large family, returned home late from work. He took one look at me:

"It looks like you lost about fifteen pounds. Eat something right away and get some rest!"

Gradually, we all settled down for tea on the ottoman. Not having to rush somewhere for the first time in many months, I told them everything that had happened in the past weeks; telephone conversations were always too brief and businesslike to do this.

It's amazing how much we had managed to accomplish in these four and a half months. And really out of nothing. From a small room in Jerusalem. We had had no base, no organization; everything was "on one foot." We just had to succeed!

It turned out that Tolik has thousands of friends throughout the world. High-placed politicians, who had met him in the Soviet Union, tourists who had visited Moscow and succeeded in becoming very close to him in two or three days, people who gained an understanding through him of what is going on in Russia—all of these people simply got up and began to speak out when they found out that he was in trouble. He was somehow close to many people; for example, that Reuters correspondent in Geneva in the U.N. press center.

Tolik's arrest, particularly after the accusation against him became known, affected Jews throughout the world. It touched hidden depths in the "Jewish soul," which the

Soviet authorities apparently hadn't expected when they devised this whole case.

Obviously they could not break Tolik. Otherwise, they would have staged a "show trial" long ago. Of the two hundred questioned in sixteen cities in the Soviet Union, not one would agree to slander him.

To this day they have not arrested anyone besides Tolik among those who were mentioned in *Izvestiya* or whose houses were searched the night before the accusations appeared in the paper. The Russians clearly did not expect such a world reaction. They were caught off guard and apparently decided to hold off until the noise died down.

The main thing was for them to understand that the noise would not die down. But what should be done next?

"Are there any plans?"

"First of all, how do you feel?" asked Ilana.

"I simply don't feel. Like a stone. My soul. And body. My muscles have become numb, as if seized by paralysis."

"Then you need some therapy. Tomorrow we'll take care of this."

We arrive at the bus station the next morning at daybreak on our way down to the Dead Sea. The yellow camelbacks of the Judean hills swim by. The sea is a blinding turquoise. Ein Gedi. I am ready to fall onto the rocks by the sea, to warm up without moving. But Ilana leads me in the opposite direction. White rocks face us in a vertical wall.

"What! You want me—as tired as I am—to climb up the mountains? I'm afraid it's not for me." And why? I couldn't believe there was anything worthwhile there but Ilana assured me that there was:

"Believe me, it's always that way in Israel: the most beautiful, the most remarkable, is carefully hidden from the eyes of a casual passerby and is revealed only to a persistent traveler. It's the same in our religion. Yes, and in our people. Let's go, it's just what you need now."

We gradually climb up along the white stone path, often stopping to rest on the warm stones. Occasionally the rocks part to reveal burbling little brooks and waterfalls. Green glades, wonderful trees, strange animals run across the grass.

These are the "sheep of Ein Gedi." They can climb trees like monkeys and walk along almost vertical cliffs. Occasionally deer appear on the path and look at us fearlessly with their large tender eyes. We could stretch out our hand to pat them.

Silence reigns. Only the rushing sound of water and the intricate singing of birds. I feel that in my chest something is beginning to melt, to calm down.

"Perhaps we can stop here. It's so marvelous."

"No, we have to go higher, to 'David's source'—he lived here when he was hiding from Saul."

The noise of the water becomes closer. Now on the right, now on the left, streams burble, forming small transparent backwaters. We pass through a tunnel which the water cut through the reeds and here we are at David's source: the green of vertical cliffs overgrown with moss, the roar of water which seems to fall from the sky. Thousands of sparkling drops like a handful of pearls strike the green-velvet wall and fall in the mirrorlike lake below. This beauty is almost impossible to bear. Something warm rises in my throat. I fall without strength. Here I can cry out loud; the roar of the water protects me, no one can hear.

After swimming in the sea and lying in the sun, we returned to Jerusalem in the evening. Ilana looked at me happily:

"You know, you got tan. The dark circles under your eyes disappeared. It's as if the day wiped the tiredness off of your face."

"That's not the main thing. The main thing is that I have begun to feel again. As if I've come back to life."

I didn't have much time to lie in bed at home. In a week I received an invitation to travel to Canada. During my brief respite, however, I understood what an enormous amount of work was going on here on this balcony and on this couch. Dozens of letters from all over the world arrived every day. We corresponded with hundreds of people from over twenty different countries. Portfolios with the history of the Shcharansky case in various languages lay on the tables and on the floor and were sent out in the mail or via travelers. People dropped by daily.

A businessman from Venezuela, who came for a vacation in Israel—yes, he could help, he had many acquaintances in the Jewish community.

A journalist from New Zealand—his articles appear in dozens of newspapers in the West.

A mathematician from America—he thinks that we must stir up the scientists.

Japanese from the pro-Israeli Makuya sect.

Students, lawyers, housewives, complete strangers, who found out our phone number from friends or through the newspaper or radio, called to offer their help. And work was found for everyone. The most important thing was for the campaign not to die down but to expand. There was no order of preference between important and unimportant; after all, one never knows from whence salvation might come.

Each day brought new events and problems. We discussed everything while drinking tea on the Turkmen carpet-sofa. We considered various plans and made decisions. From here I received support for my endless journeys.

A surprise awaited me in Canada. My lawyer informed me that he had located a branch of Tolik's family, who had not been in contact with their Russian relatives. Tolik's father's brother, who had left Russia fifty years ago, lived in the U.S. with his children and grandchildren. Here in Canada also were cousins and nephews and nieces. Many had not seen each other for years, but now, having learned about Tolik's misfortune, they banded together and became a solid force in the fight for his liberation. They received me warmly and enthusiastically. I found out that they had petitioned the Canadian government to intercede in the Shcharansky case, had written to Moscow, and organized various actions—there was no limit to their initiative and imagination.

I felt that there was "firm ground" under my feet in Canada. The work began: meetings with parliamentarians, ministers, newspaper and television interviews.

In two weeks I flew to Washington, where I was warmly received by George Meany. On behalf of the labor unions he asked Carter to intercede and promised me support in the future.

From there I flew to Stockholm, where the Swedish Parliament held a symbolic hearing of the Shcharansky case.

In October, Alan Dershowitz, a Harvard Law professor, organized a hearing of testimony concerning the case.

In November, huge declarations of protest signed by thousands of well-known people appeared in American and Canadian newspapers.

The B'nai B'rith Anti-Defamation League awarded Tolik a prize for his courageous participation in the Soviet Jewry's struggle.

During this time new forces joined the effort: the Association of Computer Technology, including thirty-five thousand members, broke off their relations with Soviet scientists. The American Academy of Sciences came out with a protest statement. The petitions of the American scientists were supplemented by signatures from 200 Swedish academicians, 136 mathematicians from Belgium, academics from Holland, Denmark, Israel, Italy, France, Mexico—over five thousand signatures in all.

The Soviet authorities were visibly upset. Crude attacks against Tolik and me began appearing. First TASS declared that I was not Shcharansky's wife, but "an agent of world-wide Zionism and the C.I.A. simultaneously." Later, a report appeared that I was not Jewish. Finally, they declared that I didn't really exist at all, I was some kind of dummied-up figure. At the same time the Moscow journal *Literaturnaya Gazeta* and Soviet overseas broadcasts reported on Anatoly Shcharansky's "moral profile," saying that he had many "lovers." On February 17, two (!) official Soviet representatives brought Senators Javits and Moynihan a letter "from my parents" which referred to Tolik as a "scoundrel and profligate." I wasn't surprised. It wouldn't be reasonable to expect courage and resolution from my parents under pressure from the K.G.B.

"Don't send us any letters," replied the senators. "Just send us Shcharansky!"

It was typical K.G.B. style to throw dirt, to blacken a reputation, to "pin on a label." But on the other hand, it resembled genuine hysterics, street language and led to the conclusion that we had, nevertheless, attained something: at any rate, they were not indifferent to what occurs in the world. Apparently they were in disarray but hoped that we could not hold up too long, the noise would die soon, and then they could quietly accomplish their planned reprisal.

I returned again to Jerusalem to "breathe a little." Changes had occurred at home in the meantime. A new headquarters appeared, of Shomer Achi Anochi (Hebrew, I am my brother's keeper). Initially, when they began to conduct demonstrations and an information campaign in Israel, they discovered that Israelis did not know that much about their brothers in Russia. Suddenly, it turned out that there was a huge interest in this subject, but no material. Everything concerning Soviet Jewry was printed either in Russian or in English; the Hebrew press contained only short bulletins, understandable only to those who followed this subject.

Michael, Ilana and Chomi decided to try to publish an information bulletin in Hebrew on the situation in Russia. The money had to be scraped together: there were always debts outstanding. They printed it in the cheapest, smallest type and mailed it to a few thousand addresses. Volunteers helped to stamp and address them. Almost every day Michael and Ilana received invitations from homes, social groups, schools and kibbutzim to come and talk about the situation in Russia, about the Shcharansky case, and about the reasons why Russian Jews drop out in Vienna. The Israelis had many questions. The number of invitations kept increasing and work on the information bulletin took up a lot of time.

Meanwhile, a nucleus grew among the volunteers. These young Sabras included the very students of Rabbi Kook who had helped us from the start. They became more and more deeply involved in the work; it added purpose and meaning to their lives. Special seminars were arranged for them on the Turkmen carpet and they gradually turned into genuine specialists, who were able to explain educational activity in Israel. The number of people increased—and the work too; the small apartment in San Simon no longer would do. Finally, we decided to separate into two branches. Our subject matter and goal would remain, as before, the liberation of Tolik, and the group of young Israelis who formed the Shomer Achi Anochi took on themselves the work in Israel. They rented an apartment for their headquarters and gradually their field of activity expanded: they began to send packages to Russia, organized correspondence between Israelis and Soviet refuseniks, collected information and news from recently arrived Soviet *olim*.

Like us, they worked without any set budget, relying on occasional donations, always in debt, operating mainly on enthusiasm.

December 15 marked nine months from the day of Tolik's arrest. We still had heard nothing about Tolik. His mother had not been permitted even one meeting with him nor had she received even a note. No one knew anything about him. Only an inner feeling, the sense I had of his continual presence alongside of me, told me that he was still alive.

According to Soviet law, nine months is the maximum term for which a person may be kept under investigation without a trial. It was natural to assume that a trial would soon begin. But we understood very well that the Soviet authorities could circumvent their own law without batting an eyelash. We were convinced of this once again when on December 16, we learned of a secret decree of the Presidium of the Supreme Soviet which extended Anatoly's detention for six months. The nature of this secret resolution, why it was taken and what it was based on were never made clear.

At the end of December, the K.G.B. demanded that Ida Petrovna find a lawyer for Tolik within a month. This could mean that the investigation was completed.

In fact, Ida Petrovna had begun looking for a lawyer for her son back in May 1977, two months after his arrest. It became evident that those lawyers who were known for their honesty did not have the so-called K.G.B. pass: they were deprived of it because they had dared to defend Nashpitz, Stern and Malkin. Nowhere in Soviet law is this "K.G.B. pass" mentioned, no one could even intelligently explain it. Nevertheless, in judicial offices they clearly understood it and lowered their eyes in fear when they heard this magic phrase.

On June 15, 1977, Ida Petrovna turned to a lawyer, Dina Kaminskaya, who agreed to take on Tolik's case. Her apartment was searched on June 19, and on the twentieth she was dismissed from the College of Barristers and told to leave the country at once. They threatened that if she would not leave, a case would be brought against her and her husband for "illegal ties with C.I.A. agents."

Over the course of a month, Ida Petrovna made the rounds of all the legal offices in Moscow. No one was willing to defend Tolik. Some blamed it on a surplus of work, others on poor health and a third group on their incompetence in such matters. A few agreed to defend Shcharansky, but only if he would acknowledge his guilt. The situation became hopeless and absurd. Finding out that any person may take his defense upon himself according to Soviet law, Ida Petrovna asked me to find a lawyer outside of the Soviet Union. The French lawyer Roland Rappaport, after questioning me in detail on all the circumstances of the Shcharansky case, agreed, received power of attorney from Ida Petrovna and immediately began making preparations to come to Russia in order to be able to familiarize himself with the material of the investigation and to be in contact with the family. They simply refused to give him a visa.

During all this time, Ida Petrovna wrote letters to the Supreme Court of the U.S.S.R., to the Prosecutor General, to the K.G.B. complaining that their son was deprived of a defense lawyer. All her complaints went unanswered. And then suddenly in December they called her in and didn't suggest, but *demanded*, that she find a lawyer immediately.

What? thought Ida Petrovna. Has something changed?

And again this aged, exhausted woman started to make the rounds of all the legal offices. And again, in turn, she appealed to various lawyers and received the same reply: no one was willing to take the risk.

The K.G.B. moved the extension to February 10, then to February 17.

They didn't even want to hear about Rappaport. No explanations, no grounds, no, and that's all!

Two American jurists who happened to be visiting in Moscow at that time, Burton Caine and Peter Liacouris, were amazed to find out about Ida Petrovna's desperate situation and decided to intercede for her. They succeeded in meeting with the chairman of the Moscow College of Barristers, Konstantin Apraksin. He had no difficulty lying to them and said that Shcharansky had a lawyer and Shcharansky's mother had already met with him several times.

On February 23, Ida Petrovna learned that the K.G.B. had designated an "acceptable" lawyer. She immediately rejected his services but no one seemed to take her declaration seriously. I found all this out through telephone conversations with Tolik's family. During that time, to my surprise, I often succeeded in breaking through to Istra.

"Natashenka, my dear, do something. They will surely kill him. Hurry, Natashenka! Only you can help, all our hopes are placed with you!"

From the other end of the world, from the darkness and horror of her life, Ida Petrovna cried; she was unable to hold back her tears.

And I hurried.

Early in February 1978, when snow covered America, I sat in Washington, D.C., in the warm kitchen of Irene and Sydney Manekofsky, Tolik's devoted old friends.

On January 20, my husband's birthday, we had picketed the Soviet embassy.

On January 27, I had attended a special reception arranged in Tolik's honor by the Coalition for a Democratic Majority headed by Senators Moynihan and Jackson.

All this was now behind us. What next?

The street was completely empty. The cars were drowning in the snowdrifts. All life was frozen. But I felt that even if the whole world was taking a rest I couldn't stop for a minute. After all, time was working against Tolik. Each day brought the terrible outcome closer.

I heard that a small group of students were planning a hunger strike for March 15, the anniversary of Tolik's arrest. Perhaps I could help them?

Maybe I could try to get as many more people as possible to join them?

"Not a bad idea," agreed Irene. We contacted Glenn Richter, chairman of the Student Struggle for Soviet Jewry.

"Excellent," he approved. "I shall work out an itinerary

for you to travel around the universities. But do you have enough strength, Avital? It will be very difficult work."

I was prepared to speak with everyone who would listen, to do everything they would ask of me—only not to sit with hands folded. The Union of Councils for Soviet Jews, with branches all over America, joined in this program. Irene's cozy kitchen turned into a coordinating headquarters. Invitations began to arrive. Calls came from universities in Atlanta, Virginia, California, Detroit . . .

In an evening conversation with Jerusalem, Ilana informed me that my brother was coming to help me. He would coordinate my trips from Washington and would try to organize support for our activities on March 15 in the House and Senate.

This period was filled with journeys by train and plane; I received more than one hundred invitations for the month remaining before March 15.

I learned to get along with very little sleep, to pack up quickly, and to rest in airplanes. But even during those brief respites on the airplane, often someone would turn up who had already seen me at one of my appearances, on television or in the newspapers. There was no place to hide.

During one of these flights, I sat next to a rosy-cheeked, middle-aged man with red hair. He looked like a real cowboy to me with his flaxen mustache, broad hat and big boots. His face expressed complete self-confidence. After crossing his feet, ordering some wine and lighting up a cigar, he introduced himself as Jimmy from Texas. Right away he told me that he was a salesman for some large pharmaceutical firm, his life was going very well in Texas—a ranch, wife, children, everything was okay.

"And where are you going? To Atlanta? On business or for pleasure?"

It was difficult for me to explain why I was going to Atlanta. I said that it was because of work with people, meetings, discussions.

"So you work with people? That's wonderful!"

He opened up his briefcase, which was full of little boxes and papers. Stopping to think for a minute, he pulled out a package of prospectuses:

"Perhaps you could hand these out to people along with my advertising samples?" he asked trustingly.

I tried delicately to explain to him that this would not suit the tone of my discussions with people. And that I was very busy.

"What kind of husband do you have," he nodded at my wedding ring, "who forces you to work so hard? And who do you leave your children with when you go on your trips?"

"I don't have any children. And my husband is very far away." Without paying any attention to me, he began discussing the modern woman, ready to neglect her children for the sake of "interesting" work. Suddenly he interrupted himself:

"How come you don't have any children? And what does that mean—your husband is far away?"

I had to explain everything to him.

The content, successful look suddenly disappeared from his face; he blushed and his eyes saddened, and genuine tears rolled down his cheeks. I asked the stewardess to bring him a glass of water.

He calmed down before the landing, and invited me to come to his ranch to rest up. He cursed the huge "Soviet prison" and promised to write to Carter. He left me only when he was sure that someone would meet me at the airport.

I had many of these episodes during my travels. Each time I melted, and thanked God that this huge, confused and often incomprehensible world contained so much goodness and sympathy.

141

                    *   *   *

Students everywhere received me very openly. I appeared
on campuses, in public auditoriums, often at mass meetings.
I established contact easily with young people; I felt that
I had never had such attentive listeners. My appearances
usually concluded with a decision by the students and often
by their instructors and professors to join in the actions on
March 15. The most active immediately formed a committee
which was in contact with the headquarters in New York.
Headquarters informed me that students in many other countries also wanted to take part in the hunger strike.

Once Michael phoned me from Washington: a report had
appeared in the American press that Dr. Sanya Lipavsky had
been a voluntary agent of the C.I.A. He had offered his
services to the Americans in the beginning of 1975; they
checked him for several months and finally rejected him
since they suspected that he was trying to establish contact
with the C.I.A. under orders from the K.G.B.

That meant that back in 1975, the K.G.B. was already
working out its terrible plan of revenge against Soviet Jews,
and Lipavsky was not simply a broken, frightened man ready
to slander himself and his friends out of fear, but a K.G.B.
agent, hiding a cold, cruel, calculating mind under his fixed
smile.

Two days later, on March 15, the anniversary of Tolik's
arrest, I stood in New York with a group of students opposite
the Soviet mission to the U.N. Pressing a small transistor
radio to my ear, I listened continuously to the latest news
summaries:

"Today,. March 15, students are conducting an international hunger strike as a sign of protest against the arrest of
Anatoly Shcharansky. Demonstrations and participants in the
hunger strike include more than one hundred American
universities, and students in England, Canada and Israel.

"During a snowstorm in Montreal, students stood for
twenty-four hours opposite the Soviet Embassy.

"Two hundred Jewish refuseniks in Russia declared a hunger strike.

"Billboards in support of Shcharansky appeared in Florida, California and Colorado.

"The American Congress declared a 'Shcharansky Day.' Seventy members of Congress delivered speeches about him.

"The legislature of the State of New York marked the anniversary of Shcharansky's arrest by a minute of silence.

"The mayors of Chicago, San Francisco and other cities read declarations of protest."

Demonstrations and protest meetings continued until June.

At the end of March, I returned home. I always left Israel in the morning and returned at sunset. Traveling back to Jerusalem, I always saw the moon rising over the city. And each time I had the feeling that I was returning after a very long working day; ahead of me was a short breathing space, and then again back to work.

Joyful news greeted me at home: Ilana and Benjamin had a new son, Ariel. Another person had appeared in our small apartment, already crowded with people and problems.

"Our ranks have been increased by a new defender of Tolik," joked Benjamin.

In the constant confusion and severe tension of our life, this peaceful little baby with his bright smile became a real safety valve for all of us.

Sometime in April the newspapers and radio reported that Shcharansky would not undergo a trial, that they would exchange him for some Soviet spy or a Chilean Communist. As a rule, the source of this news was unknown. Sometimes they brought in the utterances of some Soviet correspondent in a private conversation. At times they referred to Victor Louis, the well-known journalist of dubious reputation, whom the Soviets use to leak information when it suits them.

I was torn between a desperate desire to believe these

rumors and the fear that if I believed them I would be disappointed again. I vacillated between hope and doubt while the rumors expanded and acquired greater detail. One time the radio reported that Anatoly Shcharansky was already released and was celebrating his liberation in Moscow with a Joseph G., who was to bring him to Israel in three days. Then the report was corrected. He had not been released but would soon be released and he was not celebrating; only this mysterious Joseph G. was celebrating with the directors of the K.G.B. And yet talk continued about Tolik, about his speedy arrival in Israel, and I tried to gather all my strength, not to lose my head, not to go out of my mind from joy.

I imagined how the airplane would arrive, how he would come down the ramp, thin, worn out, how he would seek me with his eyes. And all around there would be a crowd of well-wishers, correspondents, flashes.

How could I meet him that way, in front of everyone? The television cameras would suddenly start whirring, the microphones pick up our first words.

No, I can't do it that way. I shall stay home. I'll send Ilana and Benjamin—they will steal him away.

And then I imagined it again:

There is Tolik leaving the airplane. He is exhausted, distressed, seeks me with his eyes—and doesn't find me. Instead of me there are microphones, television cameras, a crowd to greet him. No, God forbid! I shall go there. I shall find the strength. I mustn't lose consciousness from joy; even now just with the thought that it is so close, my heart is ready to burst!

The days went by. The periods of time mentioned on the radio and in newspapers passed by and Tolik did not arrive. Then new rumors spread, new hopes sprang up. I felt as if I were being burned in a fire and then right after that doused with cold water.

*　*　*

The trial of Vladimir Slepak and Ida Nudel took place in Moscow on June 21: both were sentenced to exile.

On Friday evening, July 7, it was announced that Shcharansky's trial would begin on Monday, July 10. The trial of one of the members of the Helsinki Group, Aleksandr Ginzburg, was set for the same day.

Vladimir Slepak and his wife Maria, refuseniks for eight years, were arrested for displaying a placard on their apartment balcony which read:

Give us a visa to Israel!
Let us go to our son!

The K.G.B. agents broke open the door, burst into the apartment, staged a pogrom and arrested the couple. Three weeks later in a closed trial, Vladimir was sentenced to five years of exile for "malicious hooliganism" and his wife landed in the hospital in serious condition.

The same thing happened to Ida Nudel, one of those who had been subject to a search on the eve of Lipavsky's article in *Izvestiya*. The court sentenced her, a woman almost fifty years old, to four years of exile.

It looked as if the K.G.B. had changed its original plan of destroying the Jewish dissident movement and had decided to deal with selected victims, without linking them to a "spy network" or to the Shcharansky case.

The date of the trial was clearly chosen for a reason. The K.G.B. no doubt calculated that all the zeal of the defenders of Soviet Jewry would be dissipated in protests connected with these trials and therefore wouldn't have any strength left for Tolik.

On July 7 we learned of the designated trial date and brought in a second telephone line from neighbors. We had worked out a plan of action earlier. Now we just had to agree on the final details and move into high gear. We contacted

America, England, Canada and France. The telephones weren't silent for a second.

I flew to Paris at dawn on the ninth.

In the airplane I tried not to think about how this trial might end. The most important thing now was to concentrate. To find strength in myself, as much as possible. All that I had in me.

No one had seen my Tolik for a year and a half. Tomorrow, at the trial, Ida Petrovna and his brother Lenya (Leonid) would finally see him. Perhaps I could succeed in becoming their eyes and ears? I convinced myself that tomorrow's fearful day was already not so fearful because for me it would almost be a meeting with Tolik. I wasn't at all afraid that they had broken him; I didn't need to be convinced of that. After all, I know him! He will always remain himself, under any circumstances. But how will be look? What is his mood? How is his psyche after a year and a half of solitary? Does he have any idea of how I have been living during this time? Tomorrow would bring an answer to all these questions. And now, the main thing was to keep myself in hand.

A huge crowd met me at the airport: the interviews began right away. All were friendly and attentive, but from my friends' pale faces with dark circles under their eyes, I understood how they had spent the last two days.

My lawyers held a press conference in the building of the League for the Defense of Human Rights. They read out the testimony of witnesses who had recently been sent out of the U.S.S.R. and were not able to attend the trial in Moscow.

The members of the Committee of Mathematicians were there. Thérèse Etner, chairperson of the French Committee for the Defense of Shcharansky, called on everyone to participate in the demonstration designated for the following day.

In the evening I found out that the head of the Dutch government wanted to receive me on the morning of the following day. With great difficulty, calculating each second in order not to be late for the Paris demonstration, I flew to Amsterdam.

On the airplane I gave an endless interview to the CBS television crew. At the same time Naftali, a young Israeli who had asked my permission several months ago to make a film about Tolik, and since then had been accompanying me on all my trips, got into position with his ever-present camera on his shoulder.

In the cozy small room of an old Dutch home, I had a warm, constructive conversation with the Prime Minister of Holland. And then I was back again at the airport. We almost ran to the plane. Suddenly I noticed a huge, immobile crowd by the ramp. Everyone looked at me with an encouraging smile and let me enter the airplane first. Only then did I understand that in this way the plane crew and all the passengers wanted to express their sympathy and solidarity with me. Once in the airplane, Naftali unfolded a newspaper. I saw a half-page photograph of Ida Petrovna standing by a high iron fence. We couldn't read the caption beneath the photograph, but my heart told me that she did not see Tolik today.

On the way to the demonstration I dropped in for a half hour at friends' to recover my breath. Before I had managed to cross the threshold, the phone rang: Michael Sherbourne from London. He had just spoken with Moscow, Lenya was inside, told everything to Michael in detail and now was waiting for my call at a prearranged telephone.

To my surprise, the call went through quickly.

"Well?"

"Everything's all right. I saw him. You can't imagine how calm he is. You know, I was all damp. My hands were trembling, my chin . . . And he . . . I looked at his hand when he held the paper—completely calm."

"Go on."

"The room was full of people—the trial is considered open,

147

but in fact they didn't let anyone in but me. Even Mama. Just some people with green and red passes. Not one familiar face. After the trial they took them away in buses."

"Wait, Lenka, tell me about Tolik! How does he look?"

"I'll tell you, he looks like someone who has spent sixteen months in prison. He looked at me—"

"Lenka, describe to me how he looked, where he stood. Is it really so hard?"

"He was right next to me. He smiled, said to me, 'You have gained a little weight, however.' Then, without being noticed, he showed me your picture."

"How—a picture? Where did he get my picture from?"

"I don't know. A little one, from Moscow, not from Israel."

"Lenka, you must tell him something from me tomorrow."

"That's impossible. Okay, I'll tell him. What should I say?"

"Tell him 'Shalom from Avital.' "

I heard quick, short whistles, the conversation was interrupted and I didn't succeed in talking with Lenya anymore.

My friends surrounded me. What? How? I try to tell them in coherent language what I have just heard. We run to the demonstration. From the meeting place we shall walk across town to the Place de l'Opéra. I see the faces of friends: Laurent Schwartz, Eli Artzi, mathematicians, lawyers; the crowd surrounds me on all sides. Suddenly I am encircled by correspondents, who are shoving and snapping photos. Naftali waves to me from the side, suggests that I glance back. But I already hear the growing din of the crowd. It's a little fearsome. The pressure from behind is so great that if the correspondents delayed for a minute they would simply be swept away. Gradually everyone falls into step and I hear the protesting voices:

"U.S.S.R. equals S.S.!"

"Free Anatoly Shcharansky! Free Ginzburg and Orlov!"

The windows of Parisian apartments open. People stand on their balconies and form a live corridor along the sides of the streets. Everyone has turned out—socialists and communists, the right and left, around ten thousand people are walking behind me. Nearby someone says, "Paris hasn't seen such unity since the time it was liberated from the Nazis." I lift my head to the sky. The heavy clouds part, the sun peers through.

"This is especially for you," jokes Eli Artzi, "and now stop shivering!"

On that day, July 10, at ten o'clock in the morning, the first session of the trial of Anatoly Shcharansky took place.[5] His mother was not permitted to attend the trial. Anatoly's brother Leonid, after numerous delays and checks, was led into the room and seated in the first row. About twenty out of the seventy seats remained empty. Leonid did not recognize one person.

Anatoly was quickly led in. Passing two steps away from his brother, he noticed him and smiled.

The presiding judge, Lukyanov, opened the trial. He stated that Shcharansky's mother had been given time from December 1977 to July 1978 to choose a defense lawyer. She didn't select anyone, and the inquest had been forced to invite a lawyer, Silva Dubrovskaya. The accused Shcharansky rejected the services of Silva Dubrovskaya and insisted on the right to his own self-defense. The court does not object. The lawyer Dubrovskaya leaves the room.

Immediately afterward, having received the right of counsel for the defense, Anatoly declares:

"During the whole period of the investigation, that is, for about a year and a half, they did not give me the opportunity to explain my relatives' position with regard to a lawyer. Today they declared that my mother did not want to appear at the trial."

[5] Soviet authorities, of course, did not release an official transcript of the trial. Information concerning the trial was obtained through conversations with Anatoly's brother Leonid.

Leonid screams out from his place that it's a lie, that their mother is standing by the court building and they are not allowing her to enter.

By order of the presiding judge, Leonid is reseated in the last row.

A brief pause after which Anatoly continues:

"After completion of the investigation, having taken on my own defense, I handed in a forty-page document, requesting that witnesses for the defense, various documents, books, etc., be brought to the court. The prosecutor's office took four days to familiarize itself with the materials of a year-and-a-half-long investigation, comprising fifty-one volumes, and rejected all my petitions. I am deprived of witnesses and documents which could help prove my innocence. Moreover, I am surprised that the prosecutor's office needed only four days in order to cover such a vast amount of material."

The judge questions the prosecutor on this matter. The prosecutor declares that ten minutes are enough to look this case over.

The court declares a recess.

During the recess, Anatoly contrives to show Leonid a photograph of Avital; the latter suggests with a gesture that she is fine and doing everything that she can.

After the recess the accusation is read for two hours.

Anatoly is accused according to article 64a of the Criminal Code of the U.S.S.R. of espionage on behalf of the U.S.A. and of conducting hostile activity harmful to the interests of the U.S.S.R.; and according to article 70, part 1, of anti-Soviet activity and slander.

The accusation includes in the hostile activity:

Letters and telegrams of protest with requests and demands for visas to Israel.

Meetings with senators and foreign tourists in Moscow who are labeled "agents of Zionism."

Also the letters relating to the Jackson-Vanik Trade Amendment. Here it is noted that because of Shcharansky's activity, the U.S.S.R. was not granted the status of a most favored nation in trade with the U.S.A., which affected the country's economy.

Shcharansky is also accused of slander concerning growing anti-Semitism in the U.S.S.R. and an appeal to the Conference for the Defense of Soviet Jews in Brussels.

In connection with the accusation of espionage they say that Anatoly allegedly helped compile lists of refuseniks, totaling thirteen hundred people.[6] Here, in passing, they mention the testimony of some janitor, Zakharov, who supposedly found these lists of refuseniks, written in Shcharansky's handwriting, in the garbage pail of an apartment where foreign correspondents reside.

Further on, they speak of some letter from Rubin, which Lipavsky gave the investigation, and in which, allegedly, instructions are given on how to collect espionage information. The text of the letter is not read.

The accusation according to article 70/1 of slandering the Soviet state is based primarily on documents of the Helsinki Group. These documents are referred to according to designated numerals; it is completely impossible to understand what is being said about their contents. It is said that they are "slanderous," that they "appeal for interference in the internal affairs of the Soviet Union and are useful to various subversive radio stations and publishing houses." For example: Free Europe, the German Wave, the Voice of America, the BBC *et al.*

That is all.

The judge asks Anatoly:

"Shcharansky, do you plead guilty?"

"I do not plead guilty and I consider the accusation to be absurd."

---

[6] All Jewish organizations in Europe and America have lists of refuseniks, which were never considered secret. Work on compiling them began many years before Shcharansky requested permission to emigrate.

After this the prosecutor proposes that everything connected with the accusation of espionage be conducted in a closed judicial session.

The judge asks for Anatoly's opinion.

Anatoly replies:

"Everything with which I am familiar from the materials of the investigation and everything that was read out in the accusation does not contain any secrets. I categorically object to a closed court session.

"During this year and a half of complete isolation, a tendentious investigation was conducted. Having familiarized myself with the materials in the case, I discovered that those questioned registered many complaints of being subjected to threats and pressures. Thank God that in the judicial session I at least succeeded in seeing my brother.

"Now they are planning to hold yet another closed court session. I protest. All the more so, because of all the listed accusations, the accusation of espionage seems the most absurd."

The judge declares that this question has already been decided earlier and cannot be reviewed.

Another recess is declared after which they allow Anatoly to present evidence.

"First of all," declares Anatoly, "I do not decline responsibility for any letters or documents which contain my signature and I am absolutely prepared to give evidence on every point of the accusation. But only if the court session will be genuinely open and permit my relatives, friends and representatives of the press to come into this courtroom. Otherwise, I consider it completely senseless to defend myself on each separate point of the accusation and am prepared to speak only in general terms about the problem."

Anatoly further gives an extensive picture of the situation of people who wish to emigrate from the Soviet Union. He says that since the Soviet Union has not brought its internal laws into conformity with the international documents which it has signed, all kinds of arbitrariness reign in the granting of visas and innumerable persecutions occur. He supports this by a multitude of examples. He speaks about the reasons for emigration, about the absence of centers of Jewish culture, schools, theaters and libraries.

"Who reads the books by authors who write in Yiddish?" asks the prosecutor.

Anatoly answers with a question:

"Citizen prosecutor. Did you ever bother to find out the average age of those who read in Yiddish?"

And he adds:

"Even in the Jewish Autonomous Region, there is not one school in Yiddish. I am not even speaking about Hebrew, the language of our people, who are now undergoing a renaissance. It is forbidden to teach this language, and I can name right away ten people who would like to teach it and are persecuted because of their desire."

Anatoly speaks about the recent "flowering" in the U.S.S.R. of anti-Semitism in the spirit of Stalinist nationality policies. In preparing for his defense he had requested, among other documents, two books: *The Protocols of the Elders of Zion*, whose publication had been inspired by the tsarist government and served as a background for the pogroms at the turn of the century, and a book recently published in Minsk, *The Creeping Counterrevolution*.

He had planned to show the complete identity of these books. But his request had been refused.

Moving on to the following point in the accusation about his connections with Zionist organizations and "emissaries," he says:

"Every nation passes through a formative stage of development. Now we are witnessing the historical process of Jewish renewal, of Jewish statehood, and of Jewish nationhood. So that it will be clear as I continue, I identify as Zionists those people who want to live in Israel or consider Israel as their homeland. During World War II, the Jewish Anti-Fascist

153

Committee was organized here in the Soviet Union. Through its ties with Jewish organizations around the world, the U.S.S.R. received millions of dollars in aid. No one was accused of connections with Zionists. Today, when these same organizations concern themselves with the situation of their brothers here, it is regarded as interference in internal affairs, and our appeal to them is considered subversive activity."

Replying to the accusation concerning the Jackson-Vanik Amendment, Anatoly said that the draft of this amendment was introduced back in 1972, i.e., long before he submitted documents for emigration to Israel and began to take part in the Jewish movement.

"It is not our fault that the Soviet authorities couldn't find a compromise solution such as Rumania found. The Soviet authorities' unwillingness to fulfill the obligations which they had undertaken led to the passing of this amendment."

When Anatoly moved to the document of the Helsinki Group, which was connected to the use of psychiatry and persecution for one's convictions, the prosecutor interrupted him:

"It is unethical to raise this question here as it can cause trauma to sick people."

Anatoly replied:

"If you like, we don't need to raise the question. It is enough merely to look over some of the histories of the illness, for example, in the case of Plyushch. There it is written: 'He suffers from the mania of reformism, requires further treatment.' Or another: 'Suffers the mania of emigration, needs further treatment.' And later: 'The mania of emigration has ceased, is suitable for discharge.' "

The prosecutor questioned Anatoly about his source of information for the "slanderous" documents concerning the situation of prisoners in Soviet camps. Anatoly answered that he knew about it from those who were in camps, from the relatives of those who are there now and "moreover, in the last year and a half, I have gained my own personal experience. And I have already spent time in the punishment cell."

The prosecutor asked whether Shcharansky deserved to be sent to the punishment cell.

"We are talking about conditions. By the way, I can now state the reasons for my imprisonments in the punishment cell and let the court evaluate whether it was just."

The judge interfered and requested an end to the conversation on this topic.

The prosecutor raised a question concerning the letters in defense of Malkin and Lev Roitburd:

"You write in your letter that the reason for Malkin's call-up to the army was his desire to emigrate to Israel. In fact, this is his obligation as a citizen of the U.S.S.R. since his deferment was terminated."

"You are separating the cause from the consequence, Citizen Prosecutor. Precisely because he submitted documents to emigrate, Malkin was excluded from the Institute and deprived of the right to a deferment. A man who is forcibly and illegally deprived of certain rights has the full moral right to decline certain obligations."

Anatoly also mentioned that when he had met with Albert Ivanov about this subject, he had been told that they would continue to exclude men from the institutes and take them into the army because of their desire to emigrate.

The judge remarked that no one was here who was present during this conversation.

"No, why not? I am here. Moreover, if you need to, you can call in Albert Ivanov."

The judge faltered. They turned to the following point in the accusation about the allegedly conspiratorial character of Anatoly's meetings with congressmen and senators.

Anatoly proved that these accusations were groundless. His meeting with congressmen, for example, took place in the lobby of the Hotel Sovietskaya with the participation of many correspondents. Moreover, the initiative for this meeting came from the congressmen themselves and not from him, Shcharansky, as the accusation maintains.

In no particular connection the prosecutor started a theological argument about the correctness of the religious marriage of Anatoly to Avital Shcharansky. He declared that the marriage cannot be considered valid because it did not take place in a synagogue (!) and he brings in as proof a document from Fishman, the rabbi of the Moscow Synagogue, affirming that Avital did not perform the ritual immersion in a mikvah inasmuch as if she had performed it, then she should have been called Sarah. In this connection he, Fishman, turned to the Chief Rabbi with a request to destroy the marriage certificate, the ketubah given to Avital Shcharansky in 1974 by the Moscow Synagogue.

"All this discussion is theater of the absurd and I don't intend to participate in it," said Anatoly. "The main thing is that our ketubah is signed by the rabbi and by a man whose authority in questions of Jewish law is acknowledged not only in the Soviet Union but also abroad. If I am permitted, I would be glad to invite him as a witness to give his testimony here."

They did not permit him.

The prosecutor continued:

"Look, you sent a congratulatory telegram on the occasion of the two hundredth anniversary of the United States of America, in which you declare what a just country it is, how human rights are respected there. Why didn't you mention in this telegram that America has prostitution, pornographic publishing houses and films and ten million unemployed?"

"That is true. But so much is written about all of it both in the Soviet and the overseas press that we didn't consider it necessary to mention it again. All the more so, since we live in a Soviet country and ought to speak about our own problems, about which, in our opinion, both world and Soviet society ought to be informed."

The session of the court concluded with the prosecutor declaring that tomorrow a closed hearing of the Shcharansky case would take place.

Lenya left the courtroom. The streets were jammed with people—Tolik's friends and acquaintances, foreign correspondents, representatives of the American, British, Canadian and Australian embassies. Everyone ran up, surrounded him and flooded him with questions.

A huge demonstration took place in Paris on that day.

The Israeli Knesset held an extraordinary session. At noon Israeli courts stopped work for an hour. In Tel Aviv judges went out into the streets and explained to passersby what the Shcharansky case was all about.

At Times Square in New York a huge sign was lit up: "Free Shcharansky!"

Jewish organizations all over the world sent protests to Moscow.

The next day my mood was heavy and hollow. I felt that it was because of the day's closed session. Lenya would not be able to tell me about Tolik. After speaking for a while with Jerusalem, I felt a little better.

Michael told me that Cyrus Vance was meeting with Gromyko in Geneva and that Vance had agreed to receive me. I had to go. I felt more confident when I found out that Michael Fern would come to help me, and flew the next morning to Geneva. Quiet toylike Geneva, with its little bridges and homes under sharp-edged tile roofs, had no connection with what was happening to me; it seemed like a theatrical decoration. And the activity which had to take place against the background of this decoration seemed to have no connection to it.

While I was filling out the forms in the hotel lobby, they began calling me to the telephone. The hotel began to fill up with correspondents. Everyone wanted to know the time of the meeting, but I didn't know yet myself. From time to time journalists appeared in my room and sympathetically shook their heads.

"It seems that your meeting has been put off. They will see you only after completion of the talks with the Russians." The Chief Rabbi of the Jewish community of Geneva came to the hotel, and he and his wife brought me to the synagogue, where nearly the whole community had gathered. The intense praying continued for a long time. Reporters besieged the synagogue doors while outside young people sang "Am Yisroel Chai."

In the evening, at the home of the Israeli ambassador, someone touched me on the shoulder: "Rosalyn Carter wants to speak to you." Friends were thronging around, it took a long time to make the connection. Finally I heard the pleasant, sympathetic voice of the president's wife. She expressed her support and sympathy for me and her admiration for Tolik, and then gave the receiver to Jimmy Carter's mother, and I heard her warm, supportive words.

On that day, July 12, the witnesses were questioned in the Moscow courtroom.

The first witness was the doctor of the Vladimir Prison and of a Mordovian work camp, Dr. Sukachevskaya.

She said that conditions in the prisons and camps are acceptable, that the room temperature is from 18 to 24 degrees centigrade, and that the prisoners have the right to medical service.

Sophia, the daughter of the late Colonel Efim Davidovich, appeared next. After the death of her father, who had tried for many years to obtain permission to emigrate to Israel, she and her mother had received visas and left, but they very quickly asked for permission to return. They had been allowed to return and now, no doubt, she had to pay for it. She stood for some time at the witness stand and didn't say a thing. She said that she herself would not speak and agreed only to answer questions. The prosecutor asked whether she knew Shcharansky.

"No, but I saw him twice."

"What are the living conditions like in Israel?"

She answered that she would speak only about the essence of the case and that her life in Israel was not related to it.

The judge then began to read her testimony at the preliminary hearing in a loud voice.

"No one forced the wife and daughter of Davidovich to emigrate to Israel. The director of O.V.I.R. said to her several times:

" 'You are a Russian woman and your daughter is also registered as a Russian, that means that no one discriminates against her. Then why do you want to go to Israel?' "

"At the preliminary hearing," stated the judge, "Davidovich's wife and daughter testified that the deceased man did not want to emigrate to Israel but became a victim of Zionism."

The prosecutor mentioned a letter written after Davidovich's death which was signed by sixty Jews. He asked Sophia whether it was ethical to write such a letter without consulting the family.

"No."

The prosecutor continued:

"Shcharansky and all those who signed the letter assert that Soviet authorities provoked Davidovich's death. What is your opinion?"

"That is their opinion, and I can't answer that question. But I know that my father for many years unsuccessfully requested a visa for Israel."

Anatoly was given the right to ask questions.

"Did you read your father's book, *Jews in the Red Army*, and his other works on the Jewish question?"

"No, I did not read it in Israel."

"I'm not asking about Israel. Did you read it at all?"

"Yes."

"Do you think your father was honest when he wrote this?"

The judge forbade this question.

"Did I, Shcharansky, influence your father's desire to go to Israel?"

The witness refused to answer.

All of Anatoly's remaining questions were ruled inadmissible by the judge.

During the recess, Leonid was not allowed to leave the room to see his mother, who was waiting by the door. The first witness after the recess was Irina Musykhin, Anatoly's neighbor in one of the apartments where he lived for a short time.

The prosecutor asked:

"Who came to visit Shcharansky?"

"The foreign correspondent Robert Toth came several times."

"What did Shcharansky give Toth?"

"Once I saw him give Toth forty written pages."

"Did you see what was written?"

"No."

The judge reminded her that at the preliminary hearing she had said that she had seen. But the witness didn't confirm this.

The prosecutor:

"Did Shcharansky visit Toth's apartment?"

"I don't know."

"Did Shcharansky set up a meeting with Toth over the telephone?"

"We don't have a telephone in the apartment."

"Then how did he set up meetings?"

"I don't know."

"Who else came to him?"

"Some kind of religious people."

"What did they speak about?"

"I don't know."

"Aren't you curious?"

"No, I'm not curious."

The prosecutor asked her to describe Anatoly's personality. She answered that Anatoly was well brought up, well educated and a cultured person but he dressed poorly.

The following witness was Abramov, deputy director of the personnel section of the canning factory in Derbent.

He told about an anti-Semitic meeting at this factory in 1974:

"We read the lists of those leaving for Israel and called them traitors," he explained.

"The accused slanderously affirms that there is no Jewish culture in the U.S.S.R. What can you say about that?" asked the prosecutor.

"From seven to seven-thirty there is a program in the Tat language [7] on the local radio," answered the witness.

The prosecutor turned to Anatoly:

"Were you ever in Derbent?"

"No, but my friends were there."

Anatoly asked the witness:

"Do you know how many Jews left Derbent?"

The judge forbade the question. Laughter in the room.

A man named Ryabsky appeared on the witness stand. Nothing is known about him; no one knows him . . .

The judge asked what he knew about Rubin and Shcharansky's gathering of information and their transmitting it overseas.

The witness began with irrelevant information. He declared that Rubin was a poor scholar. He said that Shcharansky was the organizer of provocative actions directed at distorting Soviet emigration policy. In particular, Shcharansky organized an illegal meeting with eight American senators. Then he spoke about the historian Professor Richard Pipes:

"He came to the U.S.S.R. as a Zionist emissary with spe-

[7] The language of the small community of mountain Jews in the northern Caucasus.

cial instructions since he is the personal friend of the anti-Soviet Brzezinski." He noted that Shcharansky's activity hindered Soviet-American relations from developing further, and that Professor Pipes gave advice on how to organize the Helsinki Group, even before the Helsinki Conference.

Anatoly asked:

"Isn't it true that the Helsinki Accords were signed in 1975, and Pipes came to Moscow in 1976?"

The witness was confused and started to explain that in fact, Pipes came to discuss the problem of the reunification of families . . .

The following witness was one Platonov from Leningrad.

He said that he didn't understand why they had brought him in, because he wasn't acquainted with Shcharansky and didn't know anything about him. He suggested that he had been brought to the trial by mistake.

Lipavsky came to the witness stand.

Judge: "What do you know about the filming of *A Calculated Risk?*" [8]

"Special emissaries of Zionist organizations secretly came to the Soviet Union, illegally made this film and took it out of the Soviet Union.

"In January 1977 the film *Buyers of Souls* was shown on Soviet television. Shcharansky and others brought the producers of this film to court, fearing that the crowd would start to lynch Jews on the streets of Moscow since their faces were now familiar to Soviet citizens." And looking straight into Anatoly's eyes, he continued pathetically:

"How can we Soviet Jews who do not want to leave live here after what you did?"

---

[8] *A Calculated Risk* was filmed in spring 1976 in Moscow by two Englishmen, the producer and director of the London studio Granada Films. A substantial part of the documentary consists of Tolik talking during a cab ride through Moscow about the situation of Soviet Jewry and about other dissidents.

The witness answered the judge's questions about the letters signed by Shcharansky:

"Shcharansky tried to place the leaders of the French and Spanish Communist parties in an awkward position by urging that they appear at the party congress with a criticism of Soviet emigration policy. He also mentioned the letters of the Jewish communities in America on the subject of separated families, letters in defense of Roitburd and Malkin, documents compiled by Shcharansky for the Helsinki Group.

Declaring that Anatoly Shcharansky tried to undermine the existing order in the U.S.S.R., Lipavsky delivered a real lecture about the interventionists' attacks in 1917 against the Soviet homeland, which were repelled. How similar attempts failed in the twenties. How the war started by Hitler ended in failure. And again, looking Tolik in the eyes, he asked:

"How could you, with your brilliant, analytic mind, believe that you could succeed where so many, in such varied historical circumstances, failed?"

Then Lipavsky again began to speak about the letters signed by Anatoly, and mentioned those connected with the Jackson-Vanik Amendment.

"Did you see me write or sign these letters?" asked Anatoly.

"No."

"Then how can you talk about my connection to these documents?"

The judge forbade this question.

This ended the court session of July 12.

My meeting with Vance on July 13 was preceded by a large press conference. I enter the overcrowded room. Hundreds of familiar and strange faces look at me. Everyone rises silently . . .

I swallow tears in my agitation, and try with all my might to control myself. I don't know what to say, in what language to say it, who will translate.

Michael Fern appears out of the crowd and without consulting anyone takes on the job of translating. I do not make any statement for the press. I simply tell what is happening at the trial, what I feel, what I plan to do. The reporters neither write anything down nor snap photos; they sit and listen. My words are followed by a long silence, then all these correspondents and journalists begin to applaud. From the audience someone calls out, "Tell us, what can we do for you? How can we help?"

"You are already helping me with your humaneness. I thank all of you for this. I hope that your readers and viewers will feel the same about what is happening now in Moscow as you do."

Later I sat next to a tall, tired man—Cyrus Vance—and asked whether he could help me. He told me that he had brought a letter from Carter to Brezhnev concerning the Shcharansky and Ginzburg trials. He, Vance, had given this letter to Gromyko and hoped very much that Anatoly would soon be released. I suddenly felt very lonely and terribly tired. Somehow I had not succeeded in making personal contact. Looking around the room, I noticed a bouquet of flowers.

"Is your wife here with you?" Mrs. Vance was called in and sat next to her husband, facing me. She greeted me warmly and smiled. As we sat and conversed in a leisurely way, one thought kept running through my mind: Shall I ever be able to sit just like that, with my husband next to me?

On that day, July 13, the prosecutor demanded fifteen years in prison for my husband.

He said that Shcharansky deserved the highest measure of punishment—the death sentence—but taking the accused's age into consideration, he was asking only for fifteen years' imprisonment.

He listed the points in the discussion based on article 64 and charged Tolik with the following:

1. Letters relating to the Jackson-Vanik Amendment and letters to American senators.
2. Documents confiscated during the search of Lipavsky's apartment.
3. Some questionnaire concerning refuseniks (no one knew what they were referring to).
4. Letters in defense of Malkin and Roitburd.

The accusation according to article 70 was based on:

1. Appeals to Jewish communities.
2. A meeting with the American historian Richard Pipes.
3. An attempt to bring the producers of the film *Buyers of Souls* to court for slander.
4. Statements concerning the death of Efim Davidovich.
5. Participation in the film *A Calculated Risk*.
6. Participation in compiling documents on the situation of prisoners in work camps and on the misuse of psychiatry.

Speaking in his own defense, Tolik declared:
"I understand that it is hopeless to defend myself in this trial, all the more so since I was accused in the newspaper *Izvestiya* a year and a half before the trial.

"I have no doubts that the court will uphold the prosecutor's request.

"There are many different systems in the modern world, but human life cannot be reduced to them alone. My social activity was interpreted as anti-Soviet and my attempts to inform the world about what is happening to Soviet Jewry as espionage."

Tolik then spoke of the rise of Zionism, of how Russian Jews, suffering discrimination and humiliation, naturally began to wish to emigrate. He recalled the Doctors' Plot, attempts at forced assimilation, prison and camps for those wishing to emigrate.

"Is this American provocation?" he asked and answered, "No, it is a historical process which can't be stopped."

Voice from the courtroom:

"They ought to hang people like that!"

Lenya recounted everything to me in the evening over the telephone. Confused, and excited, he tried to remember all of Tolik's words exactly.

Ida Petrovna had been standing for hours on end by the courtroom doors during these past three days, but they didn't permit her to enter. Tolik's father lay in bed with a heart attack.

"Do something, Natashenka, do something as fast as possible!"

I asked him whether he knew what was happening in the world.

"Only snatches."

With my voice cracking as I tried to scream to him, I enumerated:

"The day before yesterday Carter declared that this trial is an attack on everyone who believes in freedom.

"The governments of the U.S.A., France, Israel, England, Belgium, Canada, Holland, Switzerland and Italy have stated their concern and protest. As have the Communist parties of France, Italy, England and Spain.

"Demonstrations took place in New York, The Hague, Amsterdam, London, Montreal and other cities throughout the world. In Washington, for example, the president of the Lebanese League in America took part in the demonstration.

"Resolutions concerning the trial were passed by the American House and Senate. That was the day before yesterday and it is, of course, an incomplete list.

"Yesterday the governments of Sweden, Norway, Finland,

Denmark, Greece and San Marino joined in the statement of protest.

"A group of scientists in Paris declared a boycott of the Soviet Union.

"Today the Socialist International condemned the trials of Tolik and Ginzburg. Even Anwar Sadat condemns them. Demonstrations and meetings continue. New organizations, governments and political parties continue to join the protests. I don't have the energy to enumerate them all. Something inconceivable is happening! Do you hear, Lenka? Will you tell Ida Petrovna?"

On July 14, the last day of the trial, I flew to Washington at dawn. The American committee Scientists for Shcharansky invited me, paid for my expenses and worked out an itinerary for my travels around America.

When I spoke to my brother before the flight, he told me that the trial was nearing the end and when I landed in America the sentence would already be known. Friends would meet me there and I shouldn't get upset. He made me promise that I would phone home right after I landed.

"We'll already know how it ended. You must phone before you go into the hall and meet with the press."

He didn't want me to hear it from strangers, he wanted me to have some time to collect myself and recover my spirit.

In the airplane, for the first time in a long time, I was alone. During all these days, in the very thick of people and events, I had felt that I was concentrating hard, within was silence. Tolik was beside me, we were alone. And just now, when no one was near me and I had at least eight hours of flying time ahead, suddenly all the events, faces and sentence fragments rushed over me. I felt that I would drown in all this, my head was spinning: If only they would dim the lights!

Collecting my thoughts somewhat, I prepared myself for

the meeting at the airport. Who would come for me? What would I hear? The most important thing was to take myself in hand. Now it is very difficult for Tolik and me, but we are together. He is calm and collected, and I must be likewise.

The plane landed. When I reached the customs window, someone touched me on the shoulder.

"Shalom, Avital, let's go."

Simcha Dinitz, the Israeli Ambassador to America, was waiting with his wife. In its attack on me several months ago TASS had expressed amazement that this wife of the ambassador allowed herself to be photographed with Avital Shcharansky, who simply didn't exist.

"Well, I see that you still exist, and are holding up well," she smiled. On our way, the ambassador informed me that the trial had ended that morning, that Tolik had received thirteen years: three years of prison and ten in a strict regime work camp.

"Your Anatoly spoke brilliantly. He is a real hero!"

I couldn't comprehend this news. With all my understanding of what was awaiting us, I still had hoped that a miracle would occur, and that I would hear something else.

"Can I call home from here?"

"Of course."

Michael told me about the sentence, cited Tolik's final words, all in his usual matter-of-fact tone.

"We assumed that it would be that way," he said.

"Yes, but in thirteen years I will no longer be able to bear children!"

"Natasha, stop getting excited. The sentence is not everything. We shall continue to work. Nothing will stop us until Tolik is with us. We have plans. Thank God, we have the ability to find strength. Everything will be all right. Now you have to go to a press conference; collect yourself and go."

His calm, level voice instilled confidence in me. I entered

the packed room and fell into Irene's arms. Looking around at the many familiar faces, solemn and sorrowful at the same time, I couldn't control myself.

The scientists who had invited me helped me: they opened the press conference, made a statement, gave me time to collect myself. Then questions poured forth:

"Did such a demonstration really take place in Paris? Did representatives of all parties really participate?"

"What did Vance say to you?"

"How can we help Anatoly?"

Anatoly delivered his concluding words that day, turning his back to the judges and addressing his brother Leonid:

"Those who conducted the investigation warned me at the interrogations that given the position which I had taken during the investigation, the same position which I maintained during this trial, I would receive either the death sentence or a minimum of fifteen years of prison.

"They told me that if I agreed to cooperate with the K.G.B. organs in helping to destroy the Jewish emigration movement, they would give me a light sentence. They promised a speedy release and even a meeting with my wife.

"Five years ago I requested permission to leave for Israel. Now I am further from my dream than ever before. One would think that I must regret what has happened, but that is not so.

"I am happy that I lived honestly, at peace with my soul never having violated my conscience, even when I was threatened with death. I am happy that I helped people. I am proud to have known and worked with such honest and brave people as Sakharov, Orlov [9] and Ginzburg, who have continued the tradition of the Russian intelligentsia. I am happy to have witnessed the liberation of Soviet Jews. I hope that these absurd accusations against me and against all the

[9] Professor Yuri Orlov, Chairman of the Helsinki Group.

Jewish emigration movement will not hinder the liberation of my people.

"My friends know how much I wanted to exchange my activity in the Jewish movement for life in Israel with my Avital.

"My nation has been dispersed all over the world for more than two thousand years. But wherever Jews are found, each year they repeat: "Next year in Jerusalem!" And now, when I am farther than ever from my people and from my Avital, when I face many difficult years of imprisonment, I say, addressing my people and my Avital:

"*L'shana ha-baah b'Yerushalayim!*

"*L'shana ha-baah b'Yerushalayim!*

"Next year in Jerusalem!"

Turning to the judges, he added:

"I have nothing to say to this court, which must confirm an already predetermined sentence."

In a telephone conversation that evening, one of the refuseniks who had stood near the court building that day told me:

"We all gathered near the court building. The street was full of hundreds of people. Ida Petrovna continually went up to the K.G.B. men in civilian dress standing guard and asked them to let her in to hear the sentencing or at least to see her son. Sakharov also demanded that they let her in, indicating that their conduct was illegal. 'You aren't people, you are fascists!' he screamed. They still refused.

"Then two cars appeared and a small van in which they took Tolik away. We began to scream. Such a hue and cry arose from the street that one's eardrums could burst.

"Tolik's mother was weeping.

"Five minutes layer Lenya came out and said, 'Thirteen years.'

"He was in a terrible state, simply at the end of his endurance.

"He began to repeat Tolik's speech: 'Tolik said the final words twice in Hebrew and then in Russian, "Next year in Jerusalem!"'

"Then they started to lead Tolik away," he continued, "and I called out:

"'Tolik, we are all with you! The whole world is with you!'

"They grabbed me from behind by the neck and began to choke me.

"When Lenya finished talking, it began to pour but not one person left. We all sang 'Hatikvah' while the K.G.B. agents crowded around us.

"It is already night now, and I still haven't been able to pull myself together."

Letters from Prison

My dear girl, my beloved Natulya,

A whole life has passed since I sent you my last letter on March 13 of last year. If you only knew how many undelivered and unwritten letters I have sent you every day, every hour. I have relived many, many times every minute which we spent together. I constantly felt your presence. Only during these long months did I really understand what it means to enjoy your every gesture, movement, sigh and smile—everything that was and that will be.

In 1977 and 1978, July 4, the anniversary of our chuppah, were difficult days for me. But precisely on those days it was easier for me to bear any burden. I simply didn't pay attention to anything else, thinking only about you. I don't know how I could have borne everything which befell me during this year and a half were it not for you, my beloved.

Natulenka, when a few days before my arrest, I unsuccessfully tried to telephone you, sensing that this was the last opportunity to hear your voice, a "wise" man told me: "When it is very difficult for you, console yourself with the thought that it is even more difficult for Natasha." He was right—of course it is much harder for you than for me. But he was a thousand times wrong—in no way can I console myself with that. On the contrary, the one thing that oppresses and tortures me, that doesn't allow me to sleep nights, is the awareness of how difficult your life has become.

Avital, my beloved, my dear one, I believe that we shall yet enjoy genuinely happy days together—I repeat this hope every day in a prayer which I composed myself in my primitive Hebrew.

I am already dreaming of receiving my first letter from you. You have one advantage over me—you can write me every day, but I am allowed to write only once a month. Write directly to me and to my parents in Istra for me.

Where are you living now? Are you drawing? Send me a sketch of yours, Natulya.

That's all for now, my beloved.

I don't want to say goodbye, and I am not saying it—I am not separated from you for a minute.

Take care of yourself, your health and nerves. I know—to me you are a great heroine and I am very happy and proud that I have such a wife.

Greetings to all our friends—distant and close. I impatiently await your letters.

Tolya

P.S. My dears, please see that Natashenka receives this letter as quickly as possible.[1]

I kiss you all.

September 20, 1978

Shalom, my dear, my beloved Natulya,

Since I am sending two letters together this time,[2] in one

---

1 Anatoly was given the right to send only one letter per month. He addresses some of the letters to me, some to his parents. He sends the letters to Istra and his parents send them on to me.

2 Since for unknown reasons, he was not allowed to send a letter in August, he was able to write two in September.

of them I answered all of Mama's questions in detail and can therefore devote the second one entirely to talking to you. My beloved, I waited impatiently every day for the moment when I would begin to receive your letters and telegrams, but until today I hadn't received anything. My mail for two months consisted of eleven letters, all from Mama and Papa. And then, when I had just written a letter to my parents and was planning to write to you, I received my first word from you—your letter from Canada of August 28.

I immediately breathed easier.

Recently, during an exercise period, I overheard the lyrics and marvelous melody from the film *Love Story*. I had to catch my breath from memories it triggered, because this melody is also connected with an entirely different story: ours. That movie theater Warsaw in March 1974. Do you remember how deeply moved I was after the film we saw there? You were even surprised? I wasn't thinking then about the characters in the movie at all. I was thinking only about us. For some reason, I was afraid, or, more precisely, I drove away the feeling that some kind of tragedy was awaiting us. Right then I decided to persuade you to submit your documents for emigration as soon as possible, without waiting for me to receive permission.

I don't know what to call what did in fact happen, but somehow I don't want to speak about it simply as a tragedy. Our life, of course, is both more complicated and better, and more difficult and deeper than all the books and films. And how grateful I am to you, my beloved, for the joy which you have granted me in my life.

I once heard and remembered a saying that love is a special kind of advance or credit which nature (or God) gives to young people until they learn how to live with mutual cares, until they develop a mutual approach to life and its problems. You and I have turned out to be in a marvelous situation: we have not used up this credit, and my love now is not one whit weaker, perhaps even more rapturous, than five years ago. But at the same time we have matured a lot.

During this past year and a half I gained (or perhaps, more correctly, discovered for myself) many important things, recognized so many simple and evident truths, which were not easy to come by. No self-analysis, years of delving within oneself or meditation, would help me to understand myself and so much around me so deeply. It seems to me that I also understand you and have a better sense of you now than ever before. By the way, I no longer can say anything about myself without including you. Everything became so intertwined and blended that our separate lives simply do not exist any longer. I used to live through memories but now I have the sensation that we are living together; yet the times when I spoke to you over the telephone and received cassettes with your voice seem remarkable to me.

I know a little about your travels from Mama. Lenya writes that you already speak English. It's simply amazing; I was once really sure that language would be an insurmountable problem for you. Do you remember our Hebrew studies? By the way, I understood long ago that the reason for your failures was largely my fault.

Of course, I fell hopelessly behind long ago. But still, in spite of my very limited opportunities I try all the time to study some Hebrew. These studies contributed to my general health and mood during all this time.

Sometime at the end of the summer of 1977, I set myself the task of reviewing my entire stock of words. During approximately two months, I persistently recalled every word which I could somehow snatch from my memory. The total turned out to be fairly considerable—approximately two thousand words. Then I tried to bring all these words into my active vocabulary. To do this I began (and continue) to translate everything that I heard and read. Not word by word, only the general sense. Of course, this sometimes dragged out my conversations with the interrogator, but in return, I clearly attained something: in any case, I read and understood those few articles in Hebrew which were among the documents of the case. Of course there is no one to check me, but I nevertheless feel much more confident in our language than I did before.

Natulya, my beloved. You can't send me anything besides letters, postcards and telegrams, but I would very much like you to include photographs in your letters. I have one small, very tender one—Papa took it several days before your departure and it was with me all the time, during interrogations and at the trial.

As I recall, in the beginning of October Michael hit age thirty. Give him my congratulations and tell him that on that day I drank an extra mug of tea to his health.

Mama says that you dug up a whole clan or two of our relatives. Apparently Michael has shared with you his skill as an archaeologist. Convey to all the relatives my greetings and my hope to meet them as soon as possible.

This letter will probably be the last which you will receive before your birthday, Natulya. I send my congratulations in advance, my beloved, and wish that you will always be as mature and young as you have been. Another birthday without me. It is terrible to think that we were together on this day only once—do you remember, in November 1973? And then—do you remember?—we were playing chess, the first and only time in our life. We really didn't need the help of that game.

Well, that is all. I don't want to part, and I am not parting with you, my dear Avital. We are always together everywhere. I embrace you and kiss you, my joy, my pride and my happiness.

Tolya

Greetings my dear Mama, Papa, Lenya, Raya,[3] shalom my beloved Natulya!

It has been two days since I acquired a new address.[4] There is no need to get particularly upset about it—so far it has not produced any essential changes in my situation.

My dears, I beg you again and again, take care of yourselves and your health with all your might, try as much as possible not to live in that state of daily anxiety and tension which I sense from Mama's letters. You have lived such a long, hard and good life, and I dream that you will spend the last decades of your life in the warmth and joy which you so justly deserve, among your loving children and many grandchildren. But to do this you have to think more about your health and worry less about mine. I want to tell you once more, my dear old folks, that I do not simply love you, but I am very deeply grateful to you for all that you gave me and all that you taught me. It is amazing what one must go through in order to understand such simple things.

Natulya, my joy and happiness! You will probably have already passed your twenty-eighth birthday when you read this letter. Five years before that birthday marks the beginning of our life together. Although we have spent so little of these five years side by side, still, we were always together everywhere. And how good everything was that we had together.

You don't need to worry that I shall not recognize you. Mama sent me your picture with friends in Jerusalem in the summer of 1978. I constantly compare that photo of you with the little picture from Istra taken in the summer of 1974. You have lost a lot of weight. You are visibly tired. Naturally something has changed; but that something is

3 Leonid's wife.

4 Anatoly was transferred to a different prison—in Chistopol, a thousand kilometers from Moscow.

that wisdom which was given to us by these bitter years of our life and which added to your youth and beauty, my beloved wife.

During this whole time I have received only two of your letters—the first ones from Canada. And for a very long time I haven't received anything. I dream of seeing your drawings. Sketch me something or someone—Michael or Dina or Ilana with Ariel in her arms or simply some scene from our Israeli life.

I would like to hear something about Jane and Jerry, Michael, the Chudovskys, Joshua and Gladys, the Manekofskys and many, many others whom I have often thought about all this time. I won't list them all lest anyone be insulted. It's simply impossible to name them all. Of course it's hard for you to write about everyone—let others also write.

I kiss you firmly, my dear, my darling. I dream of writing you my last letter as soon as possible.

I kiss all of you, my dears.

Your son, brother and husband,

Tolya

November 14, 1978

Greetings, my dear beloved ones,

I promised to write to you on the tenth of the month, but there was a delay: they returned my letter with the explanation that I have the right to only one letter per month but in fact I write two, one to my parents and the other to my wife, who receives it via my parents. They ordered me to write either to my parents, not addressing my wife, or to my wife at her address, not mentioning my parents. To tell the truth, my first reaction was not to write any other letter but to try and get the one I had written sent, but then I thought that this could lead to new serious agitation for everyone because of the absence of a letter from me and I decided to try to meet this condition. There's no sense in writing to Natashenka's address since I have received *nothing* from her (except for the first two letters from Canada three months ago), although I know from your letters that she writes to me every day. I am therefore writing to you and I hope that you and Natashenka can fill this letter with those words and feelings which I cannot express through no fault of mine.

I am sure that Natulya will be able to fill up this letter with the bond which exists between us always and which can't be broken.[5]

December 10, 1978

Greetings, my dear beloved ones!

Unfortunately, I am writing to you again without knowing whether you received my previous letter from November.

I want to inform you right away that I shall not be able to meet with you earlier than the beginning of August 1979, since I have been deprived of my February meeting.[6]

In my new place in Chistopol, I have completely mastered my dual role of observer-participant; the critical view of the former helps the latter to live and the energy of the latter sustains the former. I have been in this situation almost uninterruptedly for the past twenty months and have succeeded in coping with it. The unbelievable sixteen-month-long tension which in my past life I experienced only for a few minutes at a time has long since left me. Although my present life appears monotonous, gray and wretched on the surface, it would be full of internal energy and movement were it not for my constant anguish and sorrow about you and for you, my dears. I can't help thinking that my beloved Natasha must spend so many of her best days, months and years in waiting, that you, my dear

5 On the margin of the letter is a sketch: Tolik's sad face.

6 Anatoly has the right to one meeting per half year. The first one took place in July, immediately after the trial. The reason for the cancellation of the February meeting has not been made clear.

old folks, may simply not have the strength. I am particularly upset about Mama, the constant tension and anxiety in which she is living are clear from her letters. Mama, I beg you, you must force yourself to live not "from letter to letter" as you yourself write, but moderately and calmly. Otherwise even your strength won't suffice for long. I beg you again and again, my dears, guard your health, and keep yourself in hand, don't get nervous because of each unpleasantness, of which, of course, there could still be many.

Please confirm your receipt of this letter by a telegram and try to convey as soon as possible my love to my darling, intelligent, dear and only Avital.

LETTER FROM IDA PETROVNA

January 13, 1979

Natashenka, my dear, my beloved, my wonderful!

Only you can understand what an overwhelming blow it was for me to receive Tolik's notification that he was deprived of a meeting. I counted each passing day after the July meeting at the Vladimir Prison and rejoiced at the approach of this long-awaited moment. I had already questioned the administration of the prison well in advance of the designated date, and prepared myself morally for the meeting and physically for the difficult journey. And suddenly everything collapsed! I have to begin counting again, but my strength dries up instead of increasing. Lenya gets angry and scolds me. He tries to convince me not to panic, but I don't think he is sincere. He says not what he feels but what he considers it necessary to say in order to reduce my sufferings. I want to see my son so much, I long for him so much and am so fearful for him and so unsure whether my strength will suffice until I meet with him! I didn't write to Tolik about this in such gloomy tones. I think I even tried to appear more or less calm and reasonable. But he is sufficiently intelligent and perspicacious and will understand my maternal game. Yes. They don't stop mocking us!

My dear daughter, Natashenka, my darling! I don't know how to pray, and I am not trained to pray to God, and therefore it is a hundred times harder for me. Pray for yourself and for me and for all of us. Tolik must be freed, it can't be otherwise! We just need to withstand, hold up and live through it!

Next Saturday, January 20, is his birthday. I remember that day, that hour, in 1948. Between midnight and one in the morning on the night of the nineteenth the persistent cry of a baby rang out and the doctor spoke:

"Mother, whom are you expecting?"

"A daughter," I said, "Natalya."

"Well, I congratulate you, you have given birth to Anatoly. That's better than Natalya," he said. "Look, what a hero!"

"But I wasn't in a joking mood, my mood was heavy and again—not a daughter, a son.

But in the morning, when they brought him for me to nurse, I melted. He was such a charming creature: round-faced, light-haired, with puffy rosy lips. He sucked greedily, tired quickly, but didn't doze. He kept looking at me with such a bright gaze that it seemed as if we had known each other for a long time and that I had never been without him. For a long, long time afterward, I couldn't forgive myself for my reaction to his birth. No daughter could ever replace my son, my Anatoly, my little hero, who grew up and became a real hero!

And then a daughter, Natalya, appeared. And all thanks to him, to my son Anatoly. And although Natalya is no longer Natashenka but Avital, she is now still dearer, closer and more beloved.

And what a nice ring these names have:

Anatoly, Natalya and Avital!

I kiss you, my dear, I love you and am always with you and with him.

I.P.

November 18, 1978
To the Senate and House of Representatives of the U.S.A.,
    Washington:
Honored Gentlemen!

Six years ago my son completed his degree in the mathematics department of the Faculty of General and Applied Physics of the Moscow Physical-Technical Institute. I remember with what enthusiasm he worked on his master's thesis and how many hopes he had for the continuation of his scientific work.

However, a year later he applied to emigrate to Israel, received a refusal and found himself a refusenik, without any rights. And during all those years, he, like other refuseniks, was subjected to arrest without trial or investigation on certain important days; he was constantly followed, and he was deprived of any opportunity to continue his research. But he persisted in his efforts to emigrate to Israel, the land of his fathers, to join his wife Avital there.

My son was arrested on March 15, 1977, and accused of betraying his country, of spying for the U.S.A., of subverting Soviet authority, of anti-Soviet agitation and propaganda and of having a decisive influence on the U.S. Congress's passing of the Jackson-Vanik Amendment.

Among the almost two hundred refuseniks without any rights who were interrogated, not one, even under pressure of threats or blackmail, would give false testimony against my son. Not one of these witnesses was called to the trial.

The authorities were forced to gather a group of known provocateurs from various cities around the country to give that absurd testimony which was demanded of them in court.

The accusation against Anatoly was so absurd and the sentence against him so unsubstantiated that the authorities have not yet permitted me or my condemned son to read it.

For a year and a half my son was in complete isolation, continually under the threat of capital punishment. He was completely deprived of juridical defense during the investigation and trial. And despite this, he kept his courage and categorically refused to cooperate with the authorities in their effort to crush the Jewish emigration movement.

My son has been deprived of liberty for many long years. But he is happy. Happy that he lived honestly, at peace with his conscience, that he helped people.

My husband and I have lived a long life. For many years we were blind and didn't understand that the place for Jews is in Israel, their historic homeland. I am happy that my son helped me, as he helped many other Jews, to understand this. No accusations of espionage, treachery or subversion will stop the Jewish emigration movement or hinder the liberation of our people.

Now we seriously fear for the health of our son. He wrote us that he continually suffers from severe headaches. His suffering is intensified by the inability to see his gravely ill father, whom he has not seen for almost two years.

In October 1978 Anatoly was transferred to the Chistopol Prison in the Tatar Autonomous Soviet Socialist Republic, a prison for ordinary criminals. After his transfer to such a distant spot, a meeting with his father became impossible.

By not giving us a copy of the sentence, they deprive us of the possibility of obtaining a review of the case and the liberation of an innocent man.

The authorities deprived my son of a defense both during the investigation and during the trial.

If my son didn't receive the death sentence, this is because the governments of many countries, the scientific community, secular and religious organizations, Jewish communities and all people of good will came to his defense.

And because the Congress of the U.S.A., with all its authority, stood up for an innocent person.

We express the most sincere gratitude for your support and hope that with your help our son will be liberated soon.

Ida   Milgrom-Shcharanskaya
Boris Shcharansky

Epilogue

A half year has passed since that day in Washington when I found out that a Soviet court had condemned me and my husband to thirteen years of waiting, loneliness and suffering.

I didn't have enough strength then to continue in America much longer; for a little more than a week, I traveled to various cities, met with people, took part in meetings and demonstrations. The American people were kind to me; they sympathized with Tolik and me, and supported us. The scientists who had invited me, who included in their number Nobel laureates and other distinguished scientists, worked out a serious program of activity in defense of my husband. Joan Baez sang for me and my husband at a huge student meeting in San Francisco. In Los Angeles, the actor Charlton Heston read Tolik's final words at the trial before a huge crowd of demonstrators.

In each city I faced meetings with scientists, press conferences, television programs. But my strength was coming to an end. One morning I simply couldn't get out of bed. I had to cancel all my planned trips and in a few days, realizing that my illness was only getting worse, I returned home to Jerusalem.

Everyone around was certain that Tolik would soon be

released. Again rumors started about an exchange. But having learned by bitter experience, I didn't give free rein to my imagination. I knew one thing for sure: I could not and did not want to become accustomed to the idea that Tolik and I were doomed to a terrible thirteen-year-long separation.

Who knows what will happen to him during these thirteen years? He has already been in a solitary cell for two years. What can be more terrible than the torture of solitude?

He is deprived of meetings with his parents.

They have forbidden him to address me in letters and my letters simply do not reach him.

He is starving. They torment him, torment him incessantly. And I? How shall I hold up during these thirteen years of nightmares, fears for him, despair and horrors?

And his parents? What will happen to them, people so dear to me, strong in spirit but old and sick?

No. I shall not concede. I shall not resign myself. Thank God, I have friends—they will not leave me. We shall continue until we shall see Tolik here, beside us.

In a press conference in Ottawa, on August 30, Irwin Cotler, my Canadian lawyer, presented an appeal which was conveyed to the Soviet authorities.

"This appeal," he declared, "was written exclusively on the basis of Soviet jurisprudence and precedents from Soviet judicial practice in order to speak with them in their own language."

An enormous amount of work had been done: dozens of people had been questioned in various countries, all the declarations of the refuseniks who had been questioned in Russia were brought together. The nine-hundred-page text of the appeal included an enormous amount of information —everything relating to the case of Anatoly Shcharansky.

Irwin Cotler discovered forty major violations of Soviet law in their treatment of my husband. (Needless to say, there were numerous minor violations as well.)

"Even one of them would have been sufficient in any normal country to release Shcharansky. They condemned Shcharansky because he took Soviet laws seriously," declared Irwin Cotler at a press conference. "Instead of honoring him for his adherence to the laws, the Soviet court declared his adherence to the laws to be a crime."

The Soviet authorities did not react at all to the lawyer's appeal.

At the same time a book came out in France, *Shcharansky: Trial Without Defense,* in which three French lawyers summed up their attempts to defend my husband against the absurd accusations brought against him at the investigation and trial.

The group Scientists for Orlov and Shcharansky, which appeared in America during the trial, has consolidated as an organization which includes the most famous American scientists. More than 2400 scientists from various universities and other places in America have joined in their campaign for a personal boycott of scientific links with Soviet scientists.

Ida Petrovna continues to strive for justice with unbelievable heroism and persistence. She writes letters to Brezhnev, the Prosecutor of the U.S.S.R., the administration of the prison where Tolik is serving his term, trying to defend her son with all her remaining strength. Her son Leonid helps her. Tolik's fate completely changed his brother's life. He had previously considered Tolik's desire to live in Israel as an eccentricity and, distant from all these problems, he often didn't understand his brother at all. Now he has taken his place. He asked me to send him, his wife and son an invitation to Israel and is waiting for Tolik's release in order to immediately submit documents for emigration.

Tolik's friends help us there in Moscow and here in Israel. Dina Beilin, who helped Ida Petrovna after Tolik's arrest, kept in constant touch with us, assembled all the information on interrogations connected to the Shcharansky case and forwarded it to us. She insisted on her right to be a witness at the trial. A short while before the trial, she received permission to leave, and to our great joy, she and her family are now in Israel. Many thought that the Soviet authorities simply threw her out before the trial in order to deprive Tolik of such a persistent and courageous witness. Dina quickly got involved in our work here in Israel.

Lunts helps us as before. Anatoly (Natan) Malkin, having served his camp term, now maturer and stronger, recently arrived here. Our ranks are growing.

Correspondence with hundreds of people all over the world continues. Sessions on the Turkmen carpet-sofa, the summing up of our experience and the working out of new plans all continue as before.

And now I am setting out again. First Europe, then America.

"This time don't return without Tolik. And try to make it as quick as possible," says Hannale as she bids me farewell.

The sun is rising above Jerusalem. People are hurrying to work. Small, independent children, with big briefcases on their backs, run to school. Mothers with strollers fill the streets and courtyards.

And I? Again—a taxi, the airport. Again desperate efforts —and what lies ahead? How will it end?

Fear overcomes me, whispers to me: "You are trying to fight against evil. It is enormous, powerful. Today it has strength. You and your Tolik don't exist for it. You can't stand up to it. You are doomed. Reconcile yourself, give up the struggle, forget that you are alive."

And then I see Tolik. I hear the level, strong voice of his letters. I see the crowded prison courtyard. The shadow-like prisoners, their hands folded behind their backs, move in a circle, and suddenly from a distance, a melody is heard. March 1974. The movie theater Warsaw. He is right, my Tolik. Our life is not simply a tragedy with darkness and despair. The melody of our love also contains the hope of much light. I remember the evening before our parting. The chuppah. The strong young voices sing:

Soon may there be heard
In the cities of Judah
And in the streets of Jerusalem
The voice of joy and gladness,
The voice of the bridegroom and the voice of the bride.

That is our melody.

The click of the teletype, the roar of tens of thousands of demonstrators behind my back: This is our melody.

Tears in the eyes of a casual passerby, smiles of encouragement on the streets of foreign cities, the dependable voices of friends—this is our melody.

In this world, where evil is on the offensive and good on the defensive, we unequivocally believe in the good.

This book doesn't have an end. Again, I am starting on my travels in order to knock on all doors, to try all possibilities. And I appeal to you, my readers. You were with me during Tolik's trial.

You sent telegrams of protest; you went out to demonstrations; you prayed for us; you supported us with your participation.

You prevented a terrible reprisal against the Jews of Russia.

Thanks to you my husband remained alive.

Each of you can do a lot. Together we are strong.

I beg you, my readers:

Help us!